TOWARDS A WESTPHALIA FOR THE MIDDLE EAST

PATRICK MILTON
MICHAEL AXWORTHY
BRENDAN SIMMS

Towards a Westphalia for the Middle East

OXFORD
UNIVERSITY PRESS

OXFORD
UNIVERSITY PRESS

Oxford University Press is a department of the University of Oxford. It furthers the University's objective of excellence in research, scholarship, and education by publishing worldwide.

Oxford New York
Auckland Cape Town Dar es Salaam Hong Kong Karachi
Kuala Lumpur Madrid Melbourne Mexico City Nairobi
New Delhi Shanghai Taipei Toronto

With offices in
Argentina Austria Brazil Chile Czech Republic France Greece
Guatemala Hungary Italy Japan Poland Portugal Singapore
South Korea Switzerland Thailand Turkey Ukraine Vietnam

Published in the United States of America by
Oxford University Press
198 Madison Avenue, New York, NY 10016

Library of Congress Cataloging-in-Publication Data is available
Patrick Milton, Michael Axworthy and Brendan Simms.
Towards a Westphalia for the Middle East.
ISBN: 9780190947897

Printed in the United Kingdom on acid-free paper
by Bell and Bain Ltd, Glasgow

CONTENTS

FOREWORD

Recent years have brought only worsening conditions in the Middle East—a continuing crisis that no-one seems to have the means or the will to resolve. In Syria the Assad regime has recovered from near-collapse in 2015, thanks largely to Russian intervention, and with help from Iran has defeated Islamic State and re-established dominance over most of the country. But that has been at the cost of many thousands of lives, and following many atrocities, including chemical attacks, against civilians by government forces and their allies. The fighting is not yet over, as rebel forces still resist. Millions of refugees are displaced within Syria and millions more have fled the country, putting dangerous strain on the delicate political, religious and ethnic balance in nearby countries like Jordan and Lebanon. Tension and fears of possible war between Israel and Iran have intensified as Israel has protested over the perception of a strengthened Iranian presence in Syria, augmented by Iran's allies, Lebanese Hezbollah.

The problems of Syria have repercussions well beyond Syria, but there are many more problems and conflicts, real or potential, in the region. In Iraq, following the latest round of civil war and the elimination of Islamic State, Shias, Sunnis, Kurds and other groups eye each other uneasily, and a lasting settlement of outstanding tensions between them seems no closer. The unresolved conflict between Israel and the Palestinians continues to fester, also affecting other regional tensions. UN officials have declared that the humanitarian crisis in Yemen is the worst in the world following the devastating bombing campaign carried out there by Saudi Arabia against Houthi rebels. Across the region as a whole Saudi Arabia and Iran accuse each other and reject the other's accusations. Beyond the region the United States and Russia align themselves with Saudi Arabia and Iran respectively, and are in turn feared and distrusted by the partisans of the other side. Sectarian hate speech and disinformation—newly defined as fake news—distort the understanding not just of ordinary people in the region and beyond, but also politicians and would-be statesmen, increasing misperception and the risk of miscalculation, and the risk of further conflict.

The problems are plainly too multifarious and interwoven to allow of simple bilateral solutions, and may seem so intractable as to prompt a feeling of hopelessness.

As historians, the authors of this volume began the Westphalia project with the observation of striking parallels between this combination of appalling suffering, fiendish complexity and apparent hopelessness, and the situation toward the end of the Thirty Years War in Europe in the middle of the seventeenth century. That war, which is thought to have cost the lives of at least a third of the population of Germany, was no less horrible and no less resistant to resolution than current conflict in the Middle East. There are many other parallels, notably the use of proxies by powers unwilling to commit themselves to war directly or to risk fighting on their own territory, and the corrosive, pervasive role of sectarian hostility (between Catholic and Protestant then, between Shia and Sunni now).

The current rivalry between Saudi Arabia and Iran, in particular, reminds me of Veronica Wedgwood's final judgement at the end of her great book on the Thirty Years War—that states and individuals seeking their own security in conditions of mistrust and fear had brought about and then prolonged catastrophic war, against their intentions:

> Yet of those who, one by one, let themselves be drawn into the conflict, few were irresponsible and nearly all were genuinely anxious for an ultimate and better peace. Almost all ... were actuated rather by fear than by lust of conquest or passion of faith. They wanted peace and they fought for thirty years to be sure of it. They did not learn then, and have not since, that war breeds only war.[1]

But the seventeenth-century parallels did not for us stop at the nature of the predicament. They offered hope of a possible resolution, because the Thirty Years War did eventually come to an end—concerted action by European states brought it to an end, with the Westphalia treaties. It was not easy, and it took a long time, but with vision, determination, flexibility and ingenuity, it proved possible to overcome the bitterness, the complexity and the hopelessness. We set about investigating whether lessons could be drawn from the success of the seventeenth-century diplomats in ending their war, for ending conflict in the Middle East now.

Immediately, in presenting our ideas, there was a recurring question we had to address. For many, Westphalia signifies the establishment of a European system of sovereign independent states, and a principle of no external interference in those states' affairs. This conception of Westphalia, though widespread and often repeated, is largely a myth (to explore the origin of the myth would be a historiographical exercise in itself, but it would seem to date to the period when nation-states became the model in Europe, in the nineteenth century). In fact the Westphalia treaties set up a system of limited and conditional sovereignty for states within Germany, with provision for appeal to courts above state level for the settlement of disputes, and for intervention by guarantor powers outside Germany in case treaty provisions were breached. In this way the reality of Westphalia is both more interesting and potentially more useful in the contemporary Middle Eastern context than this oft-quoted Westphalia myth.

A second, related point is that we are not advocating a European model for a solution to the problems of the Middle East. A large part of the problem in the region has been the failure of a European state model, imposed after 1918, that was based in part on the Westphalia myth. Our seminars showed that the real Westphalia treaties worked because they grew organically out of an inclusive conference at which parties to the preceding conflict could have their voices heard and could work together toward a solution, drawing on pre-existing legal and administrative traditions, with the help of external powers. Informal negotiating practices were at least as important in that process as formal procedures or structures. This is the central idea of the project—an inclusive peace congress at which the security needs of all parties can be heard, and addressed, and which can work toward a general settlement.

Our view is that more piecemeal solutions in the Middle East will not work, because (as in Germany in the 1630s and 1640s) the problems transcend state boundaries, are intimately interwoven and highly complex. Reaching a settlement in one state (difficult enough) will not work if that state is still destabilised by unresolved security tensions beyond its borders. A general settlement arising out of an inclusive peace congress has to be the way forward. Again, our view is that if there is to be lasting peace in the Middle East, then sooner or later it will have to happen this way.

Several participants in our seminars told us they had been asked, during trips to Middle Eastern countries, about the Westphalia treaties or the European experience of resolving confessional-based conflict. As Ralf Beste says in his preface to this book, President Steinmeier, when he was German foreign minister, was once asked this question in Saudi Arabia (Iranians have asked me the same). As he has emphasised, the idea of applying the lessons of Westphalia is an answer to a call from the region.

Underlying the Westphalia project is a conviction about the value of history as a field of study with the capability for application to problems in contemporary politics. It is sometimes useful to suggest the parallel of individual memory in this context. Would anyone try to go about their daily tasks with all memory of what had happened to them in their childhood and previous life up to, say, last week permanently erased? The idea is absurd, and impossible. Memory is essential—it makes us what we are; it is the same with history, collectively.

History is not really about dates and names. It is about the imaginative projection of the self into the position of others, as with novels and films also. This is vital because otherwise we are restricted to our own narrow experience in life. Vital because we need to be able to put ourselves in the position of others, and to understand their perspective, if we are to cooperate with them, avoid conflict with them, and enrich our understanding of ourselves and our world beyond a cripplingly low level. It is just as important for neighbours over the garden fence as it is for Saudi Arabia and Iran, to choose just two examples. And history is vital because unlike novels and films it is about What Actually Happened—*wie es eigentlich gewesen* (how it actually was)—the term used by the German historian Leopold von Ranke.

To return to the individual mode of human experience, it needs little reflection to accept that every day, when facing a new problem or a task, major or minor, our first reaction is not to start analysing or quantifying it according to first principles, but to cast back to see whether we have encountered something similar before. If we have, and we usually have, then we pursue the task according to what worked last time or, indeed, by avoiding what did not work last time. It makes sense at least to consider what a comparable method might yield when we try to deal with larger problems also, such as the problem of conflict in the Middle East. Past experience, history, may have something to tell us. Westphalia has something to tell us.

Michael Axworthy

PREFACE

Nora Müller and Elisabeth von Hammerstein,
the Körber Foundation

Four hundred years ago, the heart of Europe was devastated. The Thirty Years War, which came to be known as the first 'German trauma', has shaped the country's identity and history until today. In retrospect, several conflicts culminated in the Thirty Years War and it took three decades until the Peace of Westphalia brought an end to the protracted conflict.

Four hundred years after the outbreak of the Thirty Years War, which destroyed large parts of Europe, policy makers and experts see themselves reminded of the European catastrophe when looking at the ongoing war in Syria. What started as local protests against President Assad in 2011 rapidly evolved into a civil war and a regional conflict with repercussions far beyond the Middle East. The protracted war in Syria has damaged regional stability and has become a major point of contention between numerous regional and international powers, including Iran, Saudi Arabia, Turkey, Russia and the United States, to name but a few. The proliferation of sectarian rhetoric has further exacerbated tensions among the regional actors. Eight years into the Syrian conflict, Assad and his supporters may be winning the war, but they are still far from winning the peace. Millions of Syrians have lost their homes and lives, while the international community has been unable to unite in pursuit of ending this toxic combination of ethnic conflict, proxy wars and, above all, civilian suffering.

Both regional and external powers have been heavily criticised, including for their failure to enforce previously articulated 'red lines', thus sending mixed messages to the Syrian regime, as well as for their lack of strategic cooperation, resulting in a failure to articulate a coherent policy vis-à-vis Syria. However, while no doubt justified, none of the many critics have been able to identify a workable solution. In an attempt to contribute fresh impetus to the search for new ideas on Syria, the Körber Foundation, in cooperation with the Policy Planning Unit of the Federal Foreign Office and the University of Cambridge, initiated a project on the question of possible lessons to be drawn from the peace that ended the Thirty Years War. 'A Westphalia for the Middle East?' seeks to debate constructive approaches and creative ideas that are so urgently required in the search for peace in Syria.

Of course there are profound differences between the Thirty Years War and the conflict engulfing Syria and its neighbours. The socio-economic circumstances, Syria's and the region's unique history, as well as the complex, often fraught relationships between the respective actors demand specialised study and analysis. The analogy between the Thirty Years War and the war in Syria informing the present work thus ought to be employed as an analytical framework, and the Peace of Westphalia ought not to be used as a blueprint. Nonetheless there is value in studying history. As Samir Altaqi, director of the Orient Research Centre in Dubai, has argued:

> The contagious tragedy unfolding in the Middle East today bears a number of parallels to the problems which haunted Central Europe in the early 17th century. Once more, a diverse mix of cultures find themselves grappling with socio-economic retardation, weak cohesion, savage totalitarian regimes, widespread elite failure, fanatic ideologies, deadly vicious circles perpetuated by warlords as well as the greedy intrusion and hostile alliances of external powers. Amid this crisis, the spirit of 'Westphalia' is, in fact, a precious well of visions and experiences in terms of conflict resolution, the use of diplomatic tools, and the balancing of great-power interests.[1]

Driven by Kurt Körber's creed that it is always better to talk to rather than about each other, the Körber Foundation looks back at a long tradition as a platform for an open exchange of ideas between policy makers and experts working in and on the Middle East. Owing to the confidentiality of our discussions, participants have been able to share with one another their honest insights and opinions on current issues. Especially with regard to the war in Syria we have witnessed increasing helplessness. The foundation's approach to working on international affairs has always benefited from bringing together experts from different backgrounds and fields of expertise. The project 'A Westphalia for the Middle East?' has combined two usually separated disciplines and set a contemporary conflict in a historical perspective by using the Thirty Years War and the Peace of Westphalia as an analytical framework for the conflict in Syria and the wider region.

Over the past 18 months, the project has gathered more than a hundred experts on the Thirty Years War, as well as politicians and senior officials from the Middle East, Europe, and the US, to discuss new ideas and develop creative approaches to conflict resolution in the region. While Brendan Simms, Michael Axworthy and Patrick Milton at the University of Cambridge were able to delve deep into the roots of the Thirty Years War and the subsequent Peace of Westphalia, providing an invaluable intellectual basis, we at the Körber Foundation set out to engage policy makers and experts from the wider region to discuss some of the historical analogies as well as potential lessons to be learned—always in the hope of developing a vision of the conditions under which peace might become viable. In a series of workshops and discussions taking place in Berlin, Munich, Amman, Istanbul, Riyadh and Tehran, participants discussed the Peace of Westphalia and the question of whether elements of it might be employed in forging a Syrian peace agreement.

At a workshop in Jordan for instance, a group of policy makers and experts from the region and Europe—among them Prince Feisal ibn Al-Hussein, special assistant to the Jordanian chairman of the Joint Chiefs of Staff, and Dr Fayez A. Tarawneh, chief of the Royal Hashemite Court—discussed internal adjustments necessary for an inclusive peace settlement, such as ethnic and religious representation and legal mechanisms, which would include some form of power-sharing and decentralisation. The Peace of Westphalia had mandated parity between Catholics and Protestants at the imperial courts and other institutions, which at the time contributed to the 'juridification' of religious conflicts. It also determined that sectarian rivalries could only be resolved if all sides forwent attempts to define or impose absolute religious truth. Moreover, regulations and confidence-building measures, such as dialogue between clerics of different denominations, would have to be established to ensure peaceful coexistence despite the lack of trust.

At the Munich Security Conference in February 2017 and discussions in Berlin, Tehran and Riyadh the emphasis was put on the role of international actors and their part in a peace settlement. Commenting on the role of regional and external actors in a given peace agreement, the UN Special Envoy for Syria, Staffan de Mistura, concluded:

> the Thirty Years War provided a crucial lesson: a proxy war needs a proxy peace. Just as external powers upheld the Westphalian Peace after 1648, any sustainable peace agreement in Syria will depend on the willingness and ability of both Syrians and external actors to serve as guarantors for stability.[2]

Reactions among the discussants involved in the project varied. Whereas most found the parallels between the Thirty Years War and the war in Syria striking, unsurprisingly, the role of sovereignty in particular proved a controversial topic as it was said to have postcolonial overtones and discussants feared that it could be used to legitimise a redrawing of borders.

Regardless, using the Thirty Years War and the Peace of Westphalia as analytical frameworks to discuss policy options for Syria and other conflicts afflicting the Middle East, participants frequently were able to narrow preexisting rifts, as well as to find a more rational, constructive rhetoric with regard to their line of arguments, and hostile rhetoric was reduced.

In the pages that follow, Brendan Simms, Michael Axworthy and Patrick Milton have summarized the results of our discussions, provided a detailed account of the most important elements of the Peace of Westphalia, and outlined elements of a possible framework for peace in the Middle East. It is our hope not only to contribute to a better understanding of the Peace of Westphalia, and how it came to be, but also for it to serve as an inspiration for today's conflicts in the Middle East, especially the war in Syria.

PREFACE

Ralf Beste and Maike Thier, Federal Foreign Office of Germany

The peace congress that led to the Peace of Westphalia was the first of its kind in modern European history. It ended the Thirty Years War, a protracted, incredibly complicated and devastatingly bloody conflict; it set standards in diplomacy; and it created an order that was to last almost 150 years—and continues to have an impact on our continent to this very day, especially, of course, in Germany itself.

The interest of present-day German diplomats in this peace treaty, however, did not arise at home, where the scars and long-term consequences of the Thirty Years War can be explored in almost every town and village, but far away. During a trip to the Middle East, the German foreign minister, Frank-Walter Steinmeier, had the chance to discuss the current situation in the region with some Arab intellectuals in the Saudi port of Jeddah. It came as no surprise that the conversation quickly turned to the many crises and conflicts tormenting the Middle East. Suddenly, one of the younger participants exclaimed, 'We need a Peace of Westphalia for our region'. This comment left a lasting impression as it revealed both insight and vision. This young man was focusing on peace, not on war. 1648 appealed to him. And while history has taught us quite rightly to be wary of Eurocentrism, his invocation of an early modern European peace treaty in his personal longing for peace and a durable security architecture for his region served as encouragement: not to fear charges of parochialism, but to take seriously the potential of history in the pursuit of peace in the Middle East, even if a history of a distinctly central European kind.

Few issues have occupied the attention of the international community more than the current conflagration in the Middle East. An unspeakably brutal conflict has been raging in Syria for more than seven years. More than five hundred thousand people have lost their lives so far in this war and millions have been driven from their homes. Many of them have found refuge in Europe, not least in Germany, but even these numbers are but few in comparison with the millions of internally displaced persons who are still caught in the war zone: the millions who are sitting tight in tiny Lebanon, in Jordan or in Turkey, stretching the resources of these countries to the limit.

Syria has been a main focus of international diplomacy for years. However, despite all our efforts, we have not managed to put an end to this brutal conflict. In fact, it sometimes seems that the situation is simply going from bad to worse. It has taken us a long time to understand that this situation affects us in Europe. For this to sink in, we needed the arrival of nearly a million refugees on our own doorsteps in the heart of the continent in the summer of 2015. A series of atrocious terrorist attacks in Brussels, Paris, Nice, London, Manchester and Berlin and also in provincial Germany, in Würzburg and in Ansbach, have played a part in this, too. It has been a painful process at times but we Germans have started to comprehend that the war in Syria is not a faraway conflict but one taking place in our immediate neighbourhood.

Over time, the Syrian conflict has acquired a Gordian nature. It is too simplistic to describe it as a civil war. The true picture is much more complicated—a multi-layered tableau of actors and conflicts: a regime that is waging war against its own people; rebels of all hues, including numerous Islamist extremists; ethnic and religious minorities trapped between the fronts or, as has been the case with the Kurds, eager to seize their chance amidst the chaos and horrors of war surrounding them; the so-called 'Islamic State', a vicious terrorist organisation with no respect for human life, which murdered and enslaved people in Syria and beyond; regional powers waging a proxy war in Syria and pursuing their own interests; and, last but not least, important international actors, including Russia, Turkey and the United States, following conflicting agendas.

Foreign ministers and their staff have naturally been investing a lot of time and energy in looking for solutions to this crisis. Alongside other partners and the United Nations, the German government has been facilitating negotiations between the Syrian opposition and the regime in Geneva. We have been providing billions of euros of humanitarian assistance for refugees, we are part of the Global Coalition to Counter ISIL, we are financing the demining and subsequent rebuilding of towns liberated from IS, and we are training journalists, police and even a Syrian agency for technical relief.

While such practical help is evidently important, it is simply not enough. Yet, fresh and promising ideas for solving the conflict that really do justice to its complexities have been few and far between. As diplomats, we have always stuck by our firm conviction that military solutions will never be lasting solutions. They simply cannot be. There has to be another way. This is why Foreign Minister Steinmeier turned to history: he was convinced that it was time to go back to the drawing board and work on expanding our diplomatic toolbox.

There have been others who have compared the Syrian tragedy, this wave of violence spreading across almost the entire MENA region, to the Thirty Years War—the 'war of all wars' (in the words of the German historian Bernd Roeck). The parallels seem almost too obvious for the observer well versed in history: an uprising against a ruler, at first seemingly contained and limited, triggers a cascade of conflicts; established as well as rising regional powers exploit the situation in their quest for hegemony, driven by both a thirst for power and a fear of encirclement; governments waver as they consider how best to maintain security, by achieving territorial gains or by making political agreements; external powers foment religious conflicts to exploit them for their own ends; and finally, smaller principalities seek to expand their autonomy in the shadow of the conflicts waged over their heads.

There is a sinister side, however, to this kind of (seemingly) historically founded, intellectual commentary on the current situation in the Middle East, namely the temptation to adopt a wait-and-see attitude. The Thirty Years War is used as an excuse to show that, unfortunately, nothing can be done to alter the course of a war until all parties to the conflict are exhausted. Although such comparisons may be a welcome pretext for standing idly by, maybe even for looking away, they actually have little analytical value: in 1648, in fact, some players were exhausted while others were able to continue fighting undeterred; and indeed, they carried on, as was the case with Spain and France, just no longer within the Empire.

Politicians should therefore not succumb to the temptation to simply equate situations. History does not lay down any rules for the future. What it does, however, is to illustrate options for taking action. In the words of Margaret MacMillan: 'History, if it is used with care, can present us with alternatives, help us to form the questions we need to ask of the present, and warn us about what might go wrong.'[1] History can guide us. But it cannot determine our actions.

In a quest to identify the 'alternatives' that Margaret MacMillan pointed to, Frank-Walter Steinmeier tasked us, the Ministry's policy planners, to look for the factors that made Westphalia a success. To list just a few we found worth considering:

- One crucial factor in ending conflict is transparency regarding respective security interests—an indispensable basis for genuine peace. The early modern system of collective security established with the stipulations of Münster and Osnabrück made it possible to curb one of the main causes of conflict in the territory of the Empire, that is, fear of other countries' hegemony.
- To give such sophisticated diplomacy a chance, negotiators are needed who work discreetly and have far-ranging decision-making powers. Skilful and professional diplomats made the difference in Münster and Osnabrück.
- We need to find the strength to face up to changing realities on the ground. While peace was being negotiated in Westphalia, the war was raging everywhere else in the Empire. There was no ceasefire in place for the time of the peace congress. This, of course, in turn meant that diplomacy reacted to the changing fortunes of war. Obviously one might legitimately call into question whether we have the strength to do this in today's media age.
- Maybe the most important lesson we can learn from Westphalia is that those who seek peace cannot expect to find the full truth, clarity and justice all at once. In any war or civil war, there are always multiple truths, as told by the various parties to the conflict. That holds true today as much as then. In 1648 everyone, even the Emperor, had to make concessions in the end. They had to weigh up their interests and accept painful compromises to pave the way for peace. The negotiators wisely chose not to seek the truth of the matter but rather to focus on other, procedural matters and to use respective interests as the main lever in their efforts to resolve the central conflict.

In short, in 1648 solutions were found for some of the most pressing issues that concern us again today in the Middle East: how to disentangle religion and politics in the quest for peace; how to solve questions of hegemony; how to ensure minority rights. Nonetheless, the crucial precondition for 1648 was that there was a genuine will for peace. It needs such a readiness for compromise and openness to diplomatic solutions among the actors on the battlefield; yes, even among those whose homes have been destroyed and whose families have suffered beyond belief. And this is perhaps another aspect of the history of 1648 of relevance today: late in the Westphalian Peace negotiations a so-called 'Third Party' of Protestant and Catholic princes emerged, united in their desire for peace, not least because it was their territories and their populations that bore the brunt of the war's destructive power. We spent quite some time deliberating as to who could be the modern Third Party bringing the opposing sides together, forcing the combatants to reprioritise and to make the quest for peace the paramount consideration.

Were it just down to the desire for peace, we Europeans have obviously been ready to volunteer all along: we cannot stand the suffering and we are directly affected through the refugees. But can we really make a difference that is big enough? In all honesty, probably not. And this is why Foreign Minister Steinmeier made it his mission from the start to engage with leaders from the region, from Iran, Saudi Arabia, Turkey and other parts of the Middle East. He wanted to discuss with them what we might be able to learn from the Peace of Westphalia and which parts of the treaty of 1648 might be of relevance to today's situation in the Middle East. It is thanks to the Körber Foundation and the Cambridge Forum on Geopolitics that this discussion process was launched. Many fruitful exchanges have taken place. Importantly, this dialogue was also taken back to the region, back to where the interest in the Peace of Westphalia in the light of the current Middle East was first articulated. This book brings together the outcomes of these discussions and will hopefully serve as an inspiration for the future. After all, we are still in desperate need for a modern 'Third Party' that can create a momentum for sustainable peace.

The Peace of Westphalia is certainly not a blueprint for peace in the Middle East. But if we look at it closely enough, it offers us a number of instruments, methods and ideas of relevance for the present. It is up to us to identify these, to extract them, refine them and make use of them in our diplomacy today. This is a laborious process, but it is crucial if we want to do more than simply manage a permanent state of violence and crisis.

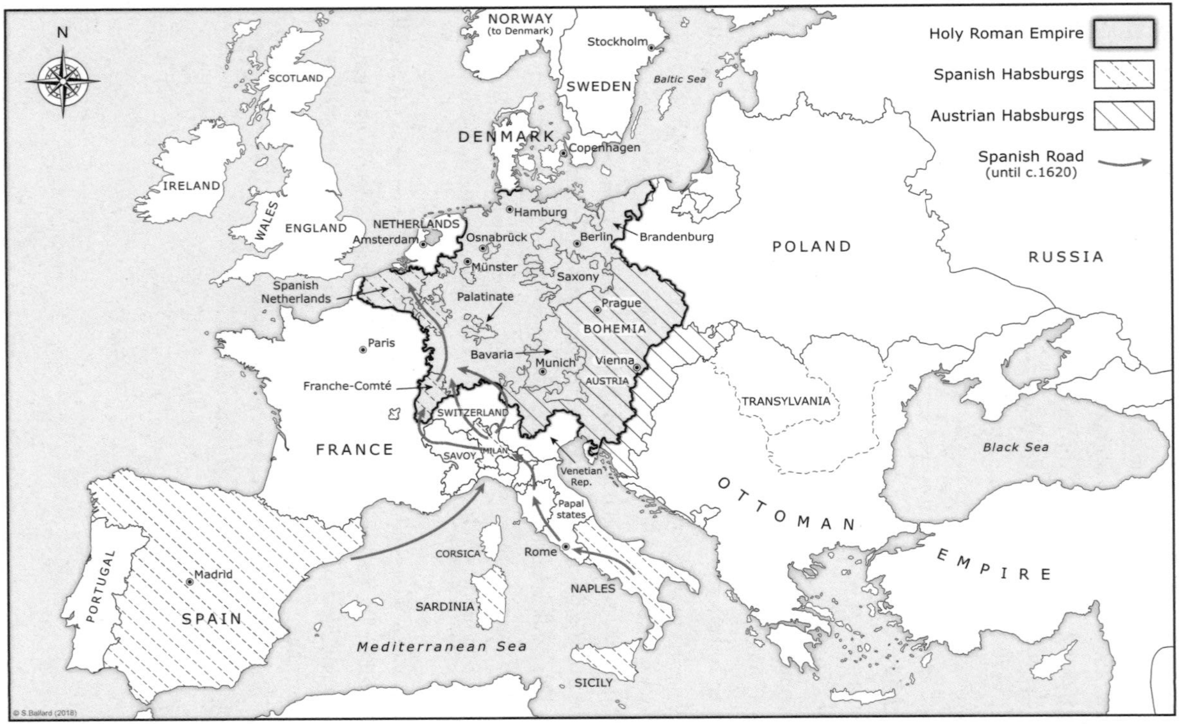
N
Holy Roman Empire
Spanish Habsburgs
Austrian Habsburgs
Spanish Road
(until c.1620)
NORWAY
(to Denmark)
Stockholm
SWEDEN
Baltic Sea
SCOTLAND
DENMARK
Copenhagen
IRELAND
WALES
ENGLAND
NETHERLANDS
Amsterdam
Hamburg
Osnabrück
Münster
Berlin
Brandenburg
POLAND
RUSSIA
Saxony
Spanish
Netherlands
Palatinate
Prague
BOHEMIA
Paris
Bavaria
Munich
Vienna
AUSTRIA
Franche-Comté
TRANSYLVANIA
SWITZERLAND
FRANCE
SAVOY
MILAN
Venetian
Rep.
Black Sea
OTTOMAN
EMPIRE
Papal
states
CORSICA
Rome
PORTUGAL
Madrid
NAPLES
SARDINIA
SPAIN
Mediterranean Sea
SICILY
© S.Ballard (2018)

Europe, 1648

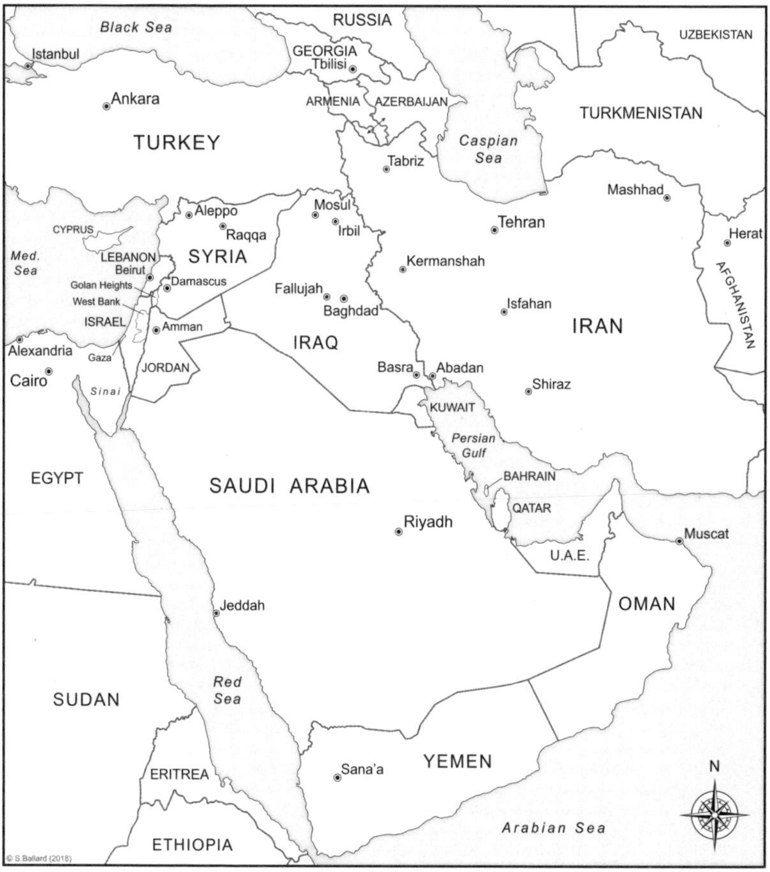

The Middle East, 2018

PART I

CHALLENGES

1

INTRODUCTION

THE RELEVANCE OF THE THIRTY YEARS WAR AND WESTPHALIA FOR THE MIDDLE EAST TODAY

Westphalia is about the idea that a regional order can be forged by its parties through negotiations that tackle the security dilemmas and meet their national and religious aspirations.

Ahmed Aboul-Gheit, secretary general of the Arab League[1]

The key idea is that coexistence between religious communities requires all sides to stop attempting to define absolute religious truth, while collective security requires a constructive and transparent dialogue on security interests with a view to reassure other parties. The peace that could ensue can be kept by guarantors, which include regional and international players that have the right to intervene in the event agreements are breached.

Raghida Dergham, founder of Beirut Institute and workshop participant at 'A Westphalia for the Middle East'[2]

The Thirty Years War and Westphalia today

A man hangs upside down in a fire. Others are stabbed to death or tortured; their womenfolk offer valuables to save their lives—or try to flee. Elsewhere, other women are assaulted and violated. In another image the branches of a tree are weighed down with hanging bodies, and a religious symbol is proffered to another victim as the last thing he will see on earth. The caption describes the hanged men as 'unhappy fruit'.

This could be Syria today—but it is Europe, in the mid-seventeenth century, at the height of the Thirty Years War. The artist who recorded these horrors was Jacques Callot, who saw the French army invade and occupy Lorraine in 1633—he was perhaps the closest his time had to a photojournalist.

Like the Thirty Years War, which was really a series of separate but interconnected struggles, recent conflict in the Middle East has included fighting in Israel and the occupied territories, in Lebanon, the long and bloody Iran–Iraq war, the two Gulf wars, and now civil wars in Iraq and Syria. As with the Thirty Years War, events in Iraq and Syria have been marked by sectarian conflict and the intervention of peripheral states (and more distant ones) fighting proxy wars. Both the Thirty Years War and the current Middle Eastern conflicts have been hugely costly in terms of human life.

The year 2018 marks the 400th anniversary of the outbreak of the Thirty Years War in Europe and the 370th anniversary of the Peace of Westphalia, which ended the war in 1648. The Westphalian peace was the result of negotiations lasting around five years at the two congress towns of Osnabrück and Münster, in the Westphalian region of north-west Germany, where the two resulting treaties were signed on 24 October 1648. Both documents, a treaty between the Holy Roman Emperor and the Empire on the one hand, and Sweden on the other, and between the former and France, constituted a single peace settlement. The preceding war was a highly complex set of events as well as being the most devastating European conflict until the twentieth century, killing between a quarter and a third of the German population.

2018 marks another anniversary, namely the collapse of the Ottoman Empire at the end of the First World War in 1918 and the partition of its Arab provinces in the Middle East by the French and the British. This colonial reordering of the region, based in part on the notorious Sykes-Picot Agreement of 1916, is often blamed for much of the subsequent malaise in the Middle East. 2018 also marks eight years since the beginning of the Arab Spring, both a reaction against and the latest stage in the region's long-term state dysfunction and turmoil. Soon after the early hopes of the Arab uprisings for greater political freedom were dashed through their degeneration into civil wars, resurgent authoritarian regimes and extreme sectarianism, the Middle East both imploded and exploded. It imploded with the collapse of core states, such as Syria and Iraq, and more peripheral ones, such as Yemen, which have all attracted proxy wars and interventions by an increasing number of rival regional powers, and this has allowed those countries to become racked by a deadly infusion and eruption of sectarian animosity. It exploded with the consequent spewing out of instability, increasing the risk of the proxies' great power patrons clashing directly, leading to the outflow of millions of refugees, and to the dispatching of bands of extremists to carry out terrorist attacks across the Middle East, in Europe and elsewhere.

These two sets of conflicts, the European one of the early seventeenth century and the Middle Eastern one of the early twenty-first century, are not usually treated together. The Thirty Years War has long been rich in both specialised studies and general accounts by historians of various nationalities. Most of these historians understandably tend to focus squarely on the historical events in order to advance a particular interpretation of history, and to discover, in the words of the nineteenth-century German historian Leopold von Ranke, 'what actually happened'.[3] Historians veering towards methodological purism have traditionally frowned upon researching the past with a view to better understanding, let alone furnishing lessons for, the present.[4] In recent times, however, the war has increasingly been cited by commentators in order to draw parallels between it and modern conflict in the present day, particularly in the Middle East and North Africa. These include a range of foreign policy practitioners, such as Henry Kissinger and the president of the US Council on Foreign Relations, Richard Haass, academics such as Martin van Creveld, and journalists such as Andreas Whittam Smith.[5] Part of the reason for drawing upon the example of the Thirty Years War is to evoke some of the horrors of that conflict, which still linger in the collective memory of at least some Europeans, especially Germans, when referring to the atrocities and catastrophes that are currently afflicting parts of the Middle East and Africa. Another reason is to advance the argument that the modes of conflict and nature of warfare have recently reverted to the kind of conflict and geopolitics that prevailed in central Europe during the first half of the seventeenth century. This is usually accompanied by the observation that recent events and conflicts are indicative of the collapse of a system of state sovereignty and non-intervention that supposedly originated with the Peace of Westphalia and that was seen to prevail from the mid-seventeenth century until recently, under the label 'Westphalian system'.[6] Increased reference to Westphalia, especially in 2017, might also be related to the unease and uncertainty that many liberal Western elites feel in the era of Trump, Putin and Erdoğan, whom they view as flouting the norms and rules of international law, undermining the international system supposedly erected in 1648.[7]

Yet this interpretation of Westphalia is largely a myth. It is a serious misunderstanding of the Westphalian treaties and their impact on international politics, albeit an extremely widespread and tenacious one. In fact, as we shall argue in this book, the Peace of Westphalia in many ways actually *reduced* the ability of territorial rulers to govern arbitrarily without external supervision and interference (at least within the Holy Roman Empire), and increased the scope of intervention in domestic affairs. However, the fact that most commentators who mention the Thirty Years War and Westphalia in the context of the Middle East tend to misrepresent the true nature of the peace settlement of 1648 does not detract from the validity and astuteness of comparisons between the Thirty Years War and the contemporary Middle Eastern crisis. Indeed, these striking parallels and analogies in many ways form the basis and vindication of our proposal of a 'Westphalian' peace for the Middle East. It is important, though, to gain a clear understanding of what Westphalia was, what it achieved, and did not achieve, if one is to consider it as a possible source of inspiration for contemporary peacemaking. The reality of the Peace of Westphalia is both more interesting and potentially more useful in the contemporary Middle Eastern context than the mythical 'Westphalian system', precisely because it is in the Middle East that the system of sovereign, equal nation-states—inaccurately attributed to Westphalia—is largely seen to have failed.

Early seventeenth-century central Europe and the early twenty-first-century Middle East

Debunking myths is not the main argument or purpose of this book, however. The idea of opening new, creative approaches for resolving conflict in the Middle East by looking at solutions that worked in the Peace of Westphalia derives from the similarities and parallels between the war that was ended at Westphalia and the current strife in the Middle East. These can broadly be summarised under two main areas: structural analogies, and the role of religion. The former broadly refers to conflict constellations, in particular the merging and confluence of various war typologies. Similar to the Thirty Years War, the current Middle Eastern crisis comprises a set of interlocking political-religious struggles at local and regional levels. The classic inter-state wars of the nineteenth and early twentieth centuries were symmetrical conflicts. Wars now, especially in the Middle East and North Africa, have returned to the kind of asymmetrical power conflicts that devastated central Europe during the first half of the seventeenth century. In both the Middle East now and the Thirty Years War then, one can observe a confusing array of different kinds of actors—states, non-state actors, sub-state actors—involved in a violent melange of different types of wars in a multipolar international environment. These include great power conflicts and rivalries, civil wars within divided and weak, or 'failed', states, confessionally infused sectarian conflicts, and rebellions or uprisings aimed at achieving greater political and religious autonomy and rights. Another important structural analogy relates to the nature of conflict progression and escalation. A comparable sequence of events occurred in central Europe after the uprising of the Bohemian nobility against their Habsburg rulers in 1618, and in the Middle East and North Africa after the beginning of the Arab uprisings at the end of 2010. In both cases hostilities began with internal rebellions, and then escalated incrementally into broader conflicts through the involvement of outside powers, starting with proxy wars, before moving on to direct military intervention. We shall argue that, as was the case with the Thirty Years War, the range of conflicts and grievances, and the array of actors in the Middle East now, are too complex and interwoven to be successfully solved with piecemeal negotiations aimed at addressing individual territorial parts of the broader regional crisis.

The second major parallel is the role of religion, which in both cases returned after its relative absence during the later sixteenth century as a major factor in conflict, and the later twentieth century respectively. Neither the Thirty Years War nor the wars in the contemporary Middle East can fully be blamed on religion or sectarianism. But both then and now, sectarian tension has tended to merge and interact with other levels of conflict.

Alternative models for the Middle East?

Deriving peacemaking lessons from the negotiations and the settlement which brought the Thirty Years War to an end is therefore a promising approach to tackling analogous conflicts in the Middle East. This is not to deny that other peace settlements and processes can be instructive.[8] A persuasive case has been made for applying to the Persian Gulf region the mechanisms and lessons from the Conference on Security and Co-operation in Europe (CSCE), which led to the signing of the Helsinki Final Act in 1975 and the establishment of the Organization for Security and Co-operation in Europe (OSCE).[9] That accord included innovative clauses such as those requiring participating states to respect human rights within their own borders.[10] It helped reduce tensions by fostering areas of cooperation. Yet in the context of the Middle East it arguably does not go far enough as a model to emulate, because it was non-binding—it did not possess treaty status. The congress of Vienna of 1814–15 and the Yalta conference of 1945, which erected post-war orders after major conflicts (the French Revolutionary and Napoleonic wars, and the Second World War), are also occasionally mentioned as possible sources of lessons for resolving today's Middle East conflicts.[11]

Yet the wars that preceded these peace conferences are hardly comparable to the Middle Eastern wars, because they were classic state-on-state wars, with clearly delineated alignments. The peace conferences of Vienna and Yalta would also be inapplicable to the Middle East without a huge escalation of violence, because they consisted of an imposition of a peace which was negotiated among the victors only, following the (expected) total defeat of the enemy. Instead of the total destruction of one side by the other, most commentators agree that the Middle East would be better served by an internationally guaranteed, negotiated peace which harmonises the security interests of as many of the involved actors as possible, while devising mechanisms to defuse sectarian animosity. This is precisely what the Congress of Westphalia achieved for central Europe in the mid-1640s. Peace settlements which sought to address individual parts of the broader Middle East conflict are potentially valuable as a model for the region as a whole. The Ta'if Agreement of 1989, which ended the fifteen-year Lebanese civil war, introduced detailed power-sharing arrangements for the various confessional groupings of that country, which are in some ways comparable to the religious terms of Westphalia. However, the resulting paralysis and virtual collapse of the Tai'f system in Lebanon are related to the fact that it was not bound into a viable regional settlement, which underlines the argument submitted in this book, that a series of intractable, interrelated and interlocking conflicts across the region need to be resolved by general settlement rather than piecemeal treaties.

Westphalia's achievements

The above-mentioned parallels and analogies—which will be explored in greater depth in later chapters—form the analytical foundation of the arguments in this book. Another reason why the Peace of Westphalia lends itself so promisingly as a potential guide towards a new settlement in the Middle East is its highly ambitious nature. It was convened as a 'universal' congress in order to achieve a 'universal peace'—*pax universalis*—between all Christian

European powers. Although it did not quite achieve this, it did successfully solve a complex nexus of conflicts in central Europe, many of which were very deep-rooted, and which seemed at the time to be insurmountable—just as insurmountable as the obstacles to general peace in the contemporary Middle East. Some of the negotiating parties never even recognised the status of their counterparts. Yet the peace in the Holy Roman Empire was achieved despite the fact that not all of the warring parties had reached a state of exhaustion, despite the fact that it became clear during the negotiations that the hoped-for all-encompassing peace covering all related wars in Europe would not be attainable—France and Spain continued fighting for another 11 years—and despite the fact that there was not even a ceasefire in place during the negotiations. The successful conclusion of the peace was deemed a 'world wonder' by contemporaries,[12] and this ambitious character of the peace congress makes its instructive potential all the more valuable.

The success of the settlement derived from several core achievements. It established new, better internal arrangements for the Holy Roman Empire, which had been the regional focus of the conflict. According to this negotiated internal set-up for the Empire, an improved form of power-sharing was established between the confessional groups (on the basis of the principle of 'parity', which obviated the risk of a tyranny of the majority), between the Emperor and the princes, and between the princes and their subject populations. These power-sharing compromise arrangements were based on the principle of the juridification of sectarian, social and political conflict. Westphalia also uncoupled the central European theatre of the Empire from the ongoing Franco-Spanish great power rivalry, which continued to be fought out elsewhere. Crucially, both the internal arrangements within the Empire and the international terms were all placed under mutual and external guarantee, thereby reshaping central Europe as a neutralised security zone under external supervision.

A 'Laboratory for World Construction' in the Middle East

Sectarianism, the interference of neighbouring powers, the breakdown of earlier state arrangements, the exodus of refugees—all of these are features of the Middle East now, as they were of Europe during the Thirty Years War, and are characteristic of a region that has become, as the satirist Karl Kraus wrote in reference to his native Austria-Hungary, a 'laboratory for world destruction'.[13] Some in the contemporary Middle East are aware of past religious extremism and conflict in Europe and ask how we overcame it historically. In a recent speech, German President Frank-Walter Steinmeier recalled a conversation with some intellectuals in Saudi Arabia, during which a young man from Syria exclaimed that what his region needs is its own Peace of Westphalia.[14] Therefore, it is in no way patronising to offer the lessons of those past traumas: it is part of our shared human experience, our collective memory. That is what history is—or can be. The Westphalia myth, in supporting a notional model of the modern state which has failed in both Iraq and Syria, may have contributed to the terrible conflicts we have seen unfolding in recent years in those countries. The real Westphalia, by contrast, could contribute to a solution.

All this requires political will and engagement, but it must begin with some intellectual legwork. To this end, the Forum on Geopolitics at the University of Cambridge established in 2015 a 'Laboratory for World Construction', drawing on expertise in both cases, to begin to design a Westphalia for the Middle East.[15] In partnership with the German think tank and non-profit organisation the Körber Foundation,[16] we have organised a series of seven major workshops and seminars (many lasting two days) in Cambridge, London, Berlin and Amman. These meetings brought together three groups of people who have hitherto operated largely independently of each other—specialists on the Middle East, historians of early modern Europe, and policy practitioners—in order to create an innovative forum for discussion. Our idea has been to explore and test the application of history, laterally and counter-intuitively, to produce fruitful debate and furnish valuable lessons for contemporary peacemaking in the Middle East. Participants included academics, journalists, retired and active politicians, diplomats and senior figures such as military officers, representing such organisations as the UN, the Arab League and the EU, as well as other institutions. Nationals from all of the main Middle Eastern states were represented.

Examples of participants include the Egyptian ambassador to Germany; the Middle East regional director of the German Foreign Office; various German and European MPs; the former Saudi deputy foreign minister; the assistant secretary general of the Gulf Cooperation Council; various officials and ministers from the Iranian foreign ministry; various officials from the German foreign office; a former Algerian foreign minister; a former Iranian ambassador to Turkey; the German ambassadors to Saudi Arabia and Jordan; the Middle East programme director of the International Crisis Group; the special assistant to the chairman of the Jordanian joint chiefs of staff; the head of the Hashemite court of Jordan; a member of the committee on foreign affairs at the Russian Federal Assembly; a former under-secretary general of the UN; a former secretary general of NATO; the head of strategic planning at the European External Action Service; several professors of history, international relations and political science; and the directors or heads of various NGOs, think tanks and research institutions including Chatham House, the Gulf Research Center, the Institute of Diplomatic Studies in Riyadh, the Institute for Middle East Strategic Studies, the American Enterprise Institute, the Institute for National Security Studies in Tel Aviv, the International Institute for Strategic Studies (IISS), the Institute for Political and International Studies in Tehran, the German Institute for International and Security Affairs, the Centre for International Peace Operations in Berlin, and the Euro-Mediterranean-Arab Association.[17]

The purpose of the project has been to look towards the peace congress and the resulting treaties of Westphalia not as a framework that needs to be followed closely, but rather as a source of inspiration for new methods of conflict resolution in the contemporary Middle East; not by imposing an external model or blueprint, but rather by trying to encourage a settlement reached by local actors themselves with the help of a toolbox of mechanisms and techniques that proved effective in the historical experience.

This book is largely a product of the discussions and debates that occurred during these workshops. It should not be seen primarily as a thought exercise of the present authors, but rather as a synthesis of the intellectual groundwork towards a Westphalia for the Middle East that has occurred as part of the research project and events series. The following chapters broadly follow the sequence of workshops that have been held so far. The resonance of the project in the region itself has been largely positive.[18] In Amman, the Jordanian government showed its support for the concept with an opening address from the King's brother, Prince Faisal ibn Al-Hussein, and an address by the chief of the Hashemite court.[19] This had been preceded by the awarding of the biennial Peace of Westphalia Prize (unrelated to our project) to King Abdullah II in October 2016.[20] The project has also enjoyed the active participation of the German Foreign Ministry. The former German foreign minister and current president, Frank-Walter Steinmeier, has taken a particular interest, giving the opening address at one of the Berlin workshops and endorsing the concept in several important speeches.[21] This, along with the 500th anniversary of the Reformation, seems to have stimulated a general interest among leading German politicians in the Peace of Westphalia over the course of 2017, when it was mentioned as a positive precursor of toleration and an admirable example of German peacemaking by Chancellor Angela Merkel[22] and the speaker of the Bundestag (parliament), Wolfgang Schäuble.[23]

The Westphalian myth

Besides works written by authors attending our project's workshops,[24] the notion of applying aspects of the Peace of Westphalia to the Middle East has been mentioned by some other authors as well.[25] While they pick up on some useful lessons, such as the value of the multilateral congress and forms of proto-toleration, their arguments were often flawed because of a fundamental misunderstanding about what the treaties of Westphalia actually were. The present book is not only the first attempt to explore this in systematic detail, on the basis of thorough historical research, but also the only such endeavour that does not fall victim to the widespread Westphalian myth. That is not to say that authors who misrepresent Westphalia have nothing useful to contribute. Often they highlight insightful parallels between the nature of warfare, conflict and geopolitics during the Thirty Years War and the contemporary Middle East.[26] The recently published, monumental book on the Thirty Years War by the political scientist Herfried Münkler, for example, provides interesting and incisive analogies between the Thirty Years War and contemporary Middle Eastern conflict, despite misrepresenting the international order that Westphalia supposedly inaugurated.[27]

That a political scientist—even one who writes a major work on the Thirty Years War—would repeat the received wisdom about the 'Westphalian system' is not really surprising, given the extent to which that myth has long been ingrained, particularly in the disciplines of political science, including international relations, but also in international law and the history of international law, and to a lesser extent in the discipline of history. It is also a standard trope among journalists[28] and politicians,[29] and has spread so widely in the popular consciousness that it has (bizarrely) even been repeated by the celebrity Katy Perry, a popular singer-songwriter, who recently lambasted the Peace of Westphalia on Twitter as the source of all evil, and in particular the evils of European colonialism, which she ascribed to the 'Westphalian' system of national sovereignty.

The Peace of Westphalia is simultaneously one of the most thoroughly researched and one of the most misunderstood peace settlements in history—albeit not by the same people! The fact that this paradox has persisted in the

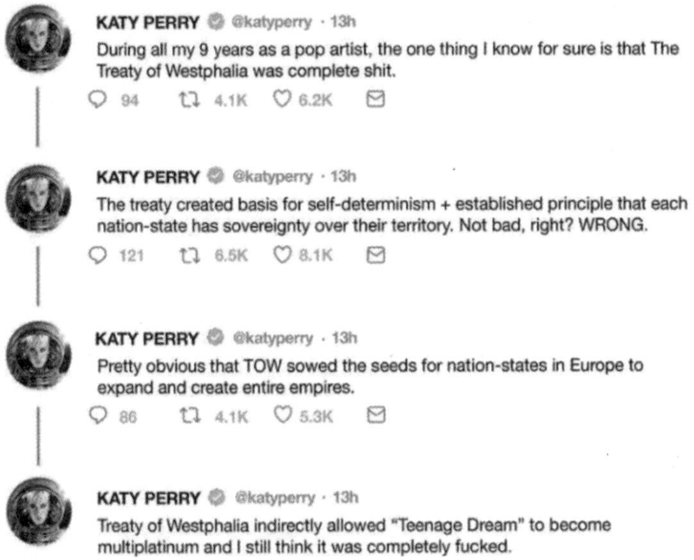
KATY PERRY @katyperry · 13h
During all my 9 years as a pop artist, the one thing I know for sure is that The Treaty of Westphalia was complete shit.
94 4.1K 6.2K
KATY PERRY @katyperry · 13h
The treaty created basis for self-determinism + established principle that each nation-state has sovereignty over their territory. Not bad, right? WRONG.
121 6.5K 8.1K
KATY PERRY @katyperry · 13h
Pretty obvious that TOW sowed the seeds for nation-states in Europe to expand and create entire empires.
86 4.1K 5.3K
KATY PERRY @katyperry · 13h
Treaty of Westphalia indirectly allowed "Teenage Dream" to become multiplatinum and I still think it was completely fucked.

last two decades, when detailed historical research into the congress of Münster and Osnabrück has been booming, is indicative of the tenacity of the myth surrounding Westphalia. The Westphalian myth consists of several assumptions and notions but these can be grouped into two main interrelated aspects. Firstly, there is the 'internal-constitutional' aspect which posits that the treaties of Westphalia granted the princes—in other words, the territories or Imperial Estates of the Empire—full sovereignty.[30] Derived from this is the 'international' aspect of the myth which assumes that the Peace enshrined the principle of state sovereignty and non-intervention in the internal affairs of other states in the broader European arena,[31] as well as the principle of the legal equality of states.[32] Related to both aspects is the notion that the Peace abolished the hierarchical elements of the European order by negating the secular and spiritual superiority of the Emperor and the Pope respectively, and instead installing the system of secular international law.[33]

As will be argued in subsequent chapters, Westphalia had very little to do with sovereignty. It neither granted sovereignty to the Imperial princes, nor did it enshrine such general principles for Europe as a whole. In many ways the individual princes and the Empire as a whole were subject to a greater degree of external supervision and intervention post-Westphalia, than before 1648.

Sovereign states existed well before 1648, and interventions in the domestic affairs of other states (and other Imperial Estates) continued well after 1648. Both the Emperor and the Pope had lost their pretensions to universal authority long before 1648. Of course we are not the first to question the traditional view of Westphalia. A rich body of research by historians,[34] international relations scholars,[35] and international law scholars[36] into the treaties and the Westphalian order, including several pieces which explicitly provide correctives to the misperceptions,[37] has nevertheless only partially dented the potency of the Westphalian myth.

In its international aspect, the myth forms the core of a model of the so-called 'Westphalian system', particularly in anglophone political science and international relations.[38] It has also become widely accepted in German and French international relations literature.[39] The notion that 1648 marks a watershed moment in international law, by enshrining state sovereignty and non-intervention, is also widespread in legal history and the international law literature.[40] The extent to which it has become a *topos* in the discipline is reflected in the titles of works which imply the belief that the retreat of the state and the growing interdependence of nations, and growing influence of transnational and sub-state actors, represent the waning of the international system erected at Westphalia.[41] Some authors even explicitly reject the careful, historical evidence-based refutations of the 'Westphalian system' and consciously reassert the myth, without, however, positing substantial supporting evidence themselves.[42] Even theorists who recognise that sovereignty was often disregarded and that interventions often occurred post-1648 still strengthen the assumptions of the myth by claiming that the principles that supposedly emanated from the Westphalian settlement have since been so systematically and extensively violated that international state practice amounts to 'organised hypocrisy'.[43] Historians have been much more sceptical about the model of the Westphalian system, but it does still appear in recent works.[44] Not all aspects of the myth are equally widespread. The argument that Westphalia ascribed full sovereignty to the German princes is more often seen in older works,[45] and is largely rejected by contemporary historians of the Empire.[46] The idea that Westphalia granted the Dutch United Provinces and the Swiss Confederation full sovereignty and independence from the Holy Roman Empire is still very widespread and has only been refuted by a small number of historians.[47]

The origins of the myth are often traced to a prominent article from 1948 by Leo Gross in which the Peace was described as a 'majestic portal' leading from a pre-modern to a modern age.[48] The foremost anglophone historian of the

Peace of Westphalia has identified the late-nineteenth-century French philosopher Pierre-Joseph Proudhon as the progenitor of the Westphalian sovereignty thesis.[49] But, as the German historian Heinz Duchhardt has argued, there is a much older version of the Westphalian myth, going back to the seventeenth century.[50] Indeed, several prominent early modern writers and theorists of the law of nature and nations, such as Gottfried Wilhelm Leibniz, Emer de Vattel and Gottfried Achenwall, varyingly viewed Westphalia as a charter for absolutism within the framework of the Empire, or as the final stage in the evolution of the Empire into an overarching system of sovereign states.[51]

Thus, the mythologising of Westphalia began much earlier than is often assumed, beginning soon after the conclusion of the Peace itself, but this version of the myth was based more on the ascription of princely sovereignty and the Empire's loss of statehood than on the inauguration of a modern state system. Picking up the arguments of the early modern theorists whom they study, modern scholars of the history of international law, especially natural law and political philosophy, often repeat the Westphalian myth, in particular with regard to natural law providing the legal ideology and justification used to attain the absolute control supposedly inherent in the Westphalian treaties.[52] The misrepresentation of Westphalian princely territorial sovereignty was continued by the Prussian and German historians of the nineteenth and early twentieth century, who sought to historically legitimate Prussia's nineteenth-century ascendancy in Germany, and thereby most likely contributed to the later emergence of the fallacy of the 'Westphalian system'.[53] Following the catastrophe of the Second World War, there occurred a fundamental German reconsideration about the desirability of a centralised unitary state capable of power projection and power accretion, a possibility which Westphalia had supposedly scuppered. From the 1960s and 1970s the Holy Roman Empire and, with it, the Peace of Westphalia as its chief constitutional law underwent a positive reassessment, culminating in the often gushing panegyrics to the Peace on the occasion of its 350th anniversary in 1998.[54] While historians have somewhat moderated their praise since then, the enthusiasm among German politicians for this instance of 'German soft power' is greater than ever.

The reason for this excursion into German and European historiography and other academic writing is to convey how entrenched this traditional fallacious view of the Peace of Westphalia is, except among small groups of historians of early modern Europe and some political scientists. Occasionally, the aim of the project of a 'Westphalia for the Middle East' has been dismissed out of hand, purely on the basis of seemingly self-evident but actually inaccurate beliefs about the Peace of Westphalia and what it stood for.[55] Experts on the Peace of Westphalia who know very well what the Peace was about, on the other hand, have occasionally criticised the concept on the mistaken assumption that a Westphalian model is being suggested for a single Middle Eastern state, such as Syria.[56] Such critiques miss the point, because the crux of the project is to explain why the Thirty Years War and the Peace of Westphalia provide valuable lessons in diplomacy and peacemaking for an analogous conflict, namely that in the Middle East. Moreover, the secondary aim of the project is not to propose a model for one particular national part of the conflict, but for the Middle East as a whole, forming the basis of a new regional order. The distinctive and important element of what is being proposed here is predicated on the realisation that all the Middle Eastern conflicts must be viewed as an interlocking overall crisis, which requires an overall solution.

Although it would be bold to claim with anything like certainty that a solution inspired by Westphalia will work in the Middle East, few, surely, would dispute that fresh ideas are needed. The potential value of a Westphalian approach (rather than a one-to-one application of specific treaty content or terms) is clear in the light of the analogous nature of strife in both cases, and the fact that the 1648 treaties successfully ended a highly complex, interpenetrating web of conflicts. But to assess whether such an approach could work, it is crucial to have a more accurate and historically informed understanding of the actual nature of the 1648 settlement and its early modern European context—one that avoids the simplistic conceptual Lego of models perpetuated in social and political science. It is understandably tempting, especially in disciplines which depend on constructing generalisable theories of international politics and history, to choose important cases as explanatory models. But detailed research by numerous historians of early modern Europe has demonstrated that the prevailing portrayal of Westphalia in political science, repeated time and again, is far from accurate and much too superficial to stand up to scrutiny.

Certain elements and claims of the myth are not complete nonsense, however. Westphalia can only be argued to have contributed towards the long-term development of the *idea* of equal sovereignty among European states (not the German princes) very indirectly, by helping to develop new practices in diplomacy and international law, such as allowing republics and the Empire's electors and princes to negotiate on similar terms with kings and the Emperor (although not on the footing of full equality in terms of ceremonial protocol). Also, although the treaties did not inaugurate a new order of international law based on non-intervention and sovereign equality, they were indeed seminal in the law of nations, by combining constitutional law with international law, and by introducing new practices such as the congress and the mutual guarantee. Although the Peace did explicitly prioritise secular law over pre-existing canon law in the case of them clashing, Westphalia cannot be described as having created a secular order (this is important because many individuals and communities in the Middle East would vehemently resist the creation of any such thing there today). Westphalia was explicitly a Christian peace, which further imprinted a readjusted and fixed confessional balance onto the Imperial constitution, and regulated relations between Catholics, Lutherans and Calvinists in a highly detailed set of confessional laws.

Strictly speaking, debunking the Westphalian sovereignty myth is perhaps not absolutely crucial to proposing a Middle East solution, because the main application we are suggesting is not of direct treaty content, but rather of methods and innovative diplomatic concepts adopted at Westphalia. The myth pertains chiefly to the content of the treaties and its impact. But there is a need to stress as clearly as possible the fallacy of the Westphalian sovereignty thesis, because if one does not know what Westphalia was truly about, the application of its lessons is unlikely to prosper. An immediate reaction to any proposed solution to contemporary problems that includes the term 'Westphalian' is likely to be that something similar was imposed on the Middle East after the First World War, and that it is precisely these arrangements, on the sovereign nation-state model, that have been to blame for many of the region's problems.[57] The mistrust of pre-cooked European models and of the sovereign nation-state model is certainly understandable, and may well be sound, but that mistrust is no reason to reject ideas derived from the real Westphalia, because, in reality, the Westphalian settlement had little to do with either.

At the heart of Europe: what was the Holy Roman Empire and why does this matter?

The Peace of Westphalia was simultaneously an international peace treaty between the Emperor and the crowns of France and Sweden, along with their respective princely allies at the end of the Thirty Years War, and a fundamental constitutional law for the Holy Roman Empire. The Westphalian treaties' peace-conserving terms and constitutional mechanisms thus applied first and foremost to the specificities of that polity. For this reason, any discussion of whether, or how, to apply lessons from Westphalia to a contemporary context requires a basic grasp of what kind of an entity the Empire was. Furthermore, the Thirty Years War was largely fought over issues relating to the constitutional, political and religious balance within the Empire. The absence or relative absence in the Middle East of such an overarching legal-political framework is relevant when considering the viability of a Westphalia for the region, although we shall argue that there are traditions and structures that could form a basis for future development and for normative consensus.

Despite an unresolved historiographical debate about whether or not the Empire was a state and, if so, what kind of state, most historians now agree on the basics.[58] It was a mixed monarchy in which power and functions of statehood and sovereignty were shared between the Emperor and the Imperial Estates. These collectively arranged themselves at three complementary levels: (1) the complex hierarchy of hundreds of Imperial Estates (princely territories or Imperial cities) at the lower level; (2) the ten regional districts ('circles') encompassing several neighbouring Imperial Estates at the intermediary level; and (3) the handful of central Imperial institutions—the Imperial Diet (assembly representing the Imperial Estates), the supreme courts (Imperial judicial tribunals—the Imperial Aulic Council and the Imperial Cameral Court), and the office of the Emperor—at the higher level. The Imperial Diet possessed legislative functions, where the various Imperial Estates—electors, princes and Imperial cities—came to a negotiated arrangement on draft treaties and resolutions relating to taxes and defence, which then needed to be approved by the Emperor. The circles were in charge of executing legislative and judicial decisions on the Imperial level, while the Imperial Estates were in charge of ruling their subjects, including the administration of territorial justice and the raising of taxes according to customary practice. The Empire can be conceived of as a hierarchical multi-level system of governance, an early modern form of consociationalism. At least among the aristocratic political and social elites of the Empire, there was a strong sense of belonging and of proto-nationhood which developed over the course of a millennium, and in which the recognition of the Emperor's overlordship was virtually unchallenged for most of the Empire's long history. The overlordship of the Emperor existed in three capacities: as the head of a *political* hierarchy of Estates, as the *judicial* apex of a legal system whereby the Emperor was the highest judge, and as the *feudal* overlord over all other fief-holders in the Imperial realm.

But the Emperor was by no means an absolute ruler over a centralised monarchy. According to the protean body of treaties, laws and customary practice collectively constituting the Imperial constitution, the numerous constituent parts of the Empire—the Imperial Estates—possessed considerable prerogatives associated with statehood. These included the ability to conduct individual foreign policies (including the right to wage war, conclude peace and alliances, dispatch embassies), and the right to rule over their subject populations. The Emperor himself was an Imperial Estate in his hereditary lands of Austria and Bohemia (the Habsburg monarchy). The elective nature of the monarchy was confirmed and enshrined in the Golden Bull of 1356, which specified that the Emperor was elected by seven of the highest-ranking Imperial Estates, the prince-electors. These rulers were the archbishops of Mainz, Trier and Cologne, the king of Bohemia, the count Palatine of the Rhine, the duke of Saxony, and the margrave of Brandenburg. The Imperial Estates were the 'immediate' subjects of the Emperor (their subjecthood to the Emperor was not mediated through any intervening lord), while the population groups within the Imperial Estates were subjects of their territorial prince, and also the 'mediate' subjects of the Emperor. These groups of subjects within the territories were often arranged into corporate entities known as territorial estates which usually, but not always, consisted of nobles, clerics or town representatives.

The nature of rule in the Empire was generally not absolutist. It was not run through centralised bureaucracies as modern states are, but was largely negotiated and carried out through personal bonds of loyalty and patronage. Corporate bodies of subjects, such as territorial estates, within most territories had considerable rights and privileges, based on positive treaty laws as well as customary practice. Often they had the right to approve taxation collected by the ruling prince. If their rights were consistently violated, any subject or groups of subjects had the right to sue their ruler at the supreme judicial tribunals, at the level which was higher than their prince in the Imperial hierarchy. If the ruler in question continued to rule tyrannically, and to ignore verdicts from the supreme courts, the Emperor could mandate an armed intervention against the offending prince for the protection of his subjects, provided this was power-politically feasible.[59]

Just as the Imperial system of limited, rights-based rule inhibited arbitrariness on the part of the princes against their subjects, so it prevented arbitrary rule by the Emperor over his immediate subjects, the princes. These also had considerable rights and privileges based in treaty and customary law, the famous 'German liberties', which primarily related to their right to share in the government and management of the Empire. Rights were generally not universal and individual, as they are conceptualised today, but rather corporate—in other words, attached to certain groups with a recognised status. Indeed, one of the chief functions of the Empire was the mutual protection of these corporate rights. Thus the Empire was a highly decentralised system, based on checks and balances, and structurally incapable of aggressive external power projection and expansion. Instead it was an association of heterogeneous corporate parts geared towards mutual defence.[60] At the end of the fifteenth century the elites of the Empire completed a reform process which restructured the Empire as a defensive order of peace and legality. In 1495 an Eternal Territorial Peace was declared in which the use of force was henceforth banned within the Empire, unless mandated by the newly established Imperial judiciary. All members of the Empire were placed under the protective umbrella of this Eternal Peace. Contrary to how the Empire used to be portrayed, its members were capable of reforming and adapting their set-up until the late eighteenth century, which in part accounts for its thousand-year-long survival.[61]

The most important conclusion of this overview is that the Empire was a system based on tradition and legality, and that this system depended for its smooth functioning on a high degree of cooperation, consensus and the willingness to compromise on the part of its constituent political parts. It was precisely this willingness to compromise, cooperate and seek consensus which broke down in the decades leading up to the outbreak of the Thirty Years War.

Before addressing that conflict, the next chapter will address the nature of the Middle East crisis of recent years, the set of conflicts that require a fresh perspective towards a solution. The following two chapters, which constitute Part II, will delve into the European historical background in depth, while highlighting the relevant parallels to the Middle East. They will address the causes of the outbreak of the Thirty Years War and the origins of the war's incremental escalation. The ways in which peace was finally achieved will then be set out, and an explanation of why it took so long to end the war and to achieve peace will be proffered. The impact of the Peace of Westphalia in the subsequent period will also be addressed. In the two final chapters, which form Part III, we then shift towards the explicitly applicatory part of the book. We will first systematically expound the parallels and analogies between the Thirty Years War and the contemporary Middle East. We then turn to the two main kinds of lessons that can be drawn for the benefit of peace in the Middle East, namely diplomatic techniques and mechanisms on the one hand, and treaty content on the other. Finally we suggest the broad outlines of a new Westphalian regional order for the Middle East.

2

CHALLENGES AND CRISES IN THE MIDDLE EAST

In a most dramatic fashion, history is compelling us to bear witness once more to the agonizing process of a region falling apart and reassembling its constituent pieces. The contagious tragedy unfolding in the Middle East today bears a number of parallels to the problems which haunted central Europe in the early seventeenth century. Once more, a diverse mix of cultures find themselves grappling with socio-economic retardation, weak cohesion, savage totalitarian regimes, widespread elite failure, fanatic ideologies, deadly vicious circles perpetuated by warlords as well as the greedy intrusion and hostile alliances of external powers. Amid this crisis, the spirit of 'Westphalia' is, in fact, a precious well of visions and experiences in terms of conflict resolution, the use of diplomatic tools, and the balancing of great-power interests.

Samir Altaqi, director general, Orient Research Centre, Dubai, workshop participant of 'A Westphalia for the Middle East?', 2016–17[1]

The Peace of Westphalia, which ended the Thirty Years War in 1648, has provided enduring lessons for similar endeavours ever since. In view of that, [it is helpful to] revisit that endeavour for insights that might help guide development of creative approaches to resolving the conflicts in Syria and the greater Middle East.

General David H. Petraeus, former CIA director[2]

The conflicts and crises in the Middle East show no sign of abating.[3] The Syrian civil war—the prime focus of the regional trauma—has killed as many as half a million people since its beginning in 2011, and has displaced many millions more, both internally and as cross-border refugees seeking shelter in Lebanon, Turkey, Europe and elsewhere. Intervening powers continue to prop up and fund a barbaric government as well as a plethora of proxies on the ground, and to conduct direct military interventions. In Yemen, the other major 'hot' conflict in the region marked by extensive internationalisation and intervention, around ten thousand people, mainly civilians, have been killed as a direct result of military operations since 2015, and many more as an indirect result of the fighting, through disease and starvation. Although government forces and allied militias in Iraq, together with their foreign sponsors and helpers, have reconquered large swathes of territory from the Islamic State (and from Kurdish separatists following a failed independence referendum in September 2017), it remains a vulnerable and unstable polity, its weakness and instability similarly attracting the involvement of regional and global powers. The situation in Lebanon, where the Iranian-backed Hezbollah calls the shots, is similarly tense, and the same can be said of Libya, which is divided between warring rival governments, each backed by different foreign patrons. The fate of all of these countries seems to be largely or totally out of the hands of their nominal governments and of their inhabitants.

Other states in the region which have been less severely affected by external intervention have also experienced serious domestic instability or peril from foreign powers. Egypt has been destabilised by a revolution and a military coup in 2011–13 in rapid succession, leading to the return of an autocratic regime even more repressive than before. Turkey's authoritarian president saw off an attempted military coup d'état in 2016 and has since expanded his powers while clamping down on dissent and stifling civil liberties. Saudi Arabia experienced a purge following a power grab by an ambitious new crown prince in 2017, while accusing its great regional rival, Iran, of having committed acts of war against it by proxy in Yemen. Iran in turn has been shaken by domestic popular anti-government unrest—which, though mainly motivated by economic trauma, included protests against the Islamic Republic's expensive foreign adventures—and the Iranian regime in turn blamed Saudi Arabia (among others) for instigating the protests. Qatar has faced off an unprecedented Saudi-led multilateral blockade since mid-2017 and stood up against an ultimatum designed to force it to submit to Saudi leadership among Sunni regional powers. Terrorist outrages remain grimly commonplace in many parts of the region.

At first sight these various wars, cold wars and crises appear as distinct conflicts. Yet a closer analysis reveals that they are in fact profoundly interconnected, and that these connections point towards a single regional crisis afflicting the Middle East. The purpose of this book and the research project upon which it is based is to draw lessons from the Thirty Years War and the Peace of Westphalia which ended it. Part of the value of this exercise derives from the possibility of examining analogous historical processes in order to help us better understand current events that are still unfolding. It was tempting for people to regard the Thirty Years War as a series of discrete events and wars, yet more astute contemporary observers and historians since then have recognised the interlocking nature of the problems and have seen in it a single crisis and war with its own causes, course and consequences. This insight helps us to recognise the various comparable crises and conflicts of the Middle East today as being part of a single regional event encompassing Iran and the non-European post-Ottoman space, namely Turkey, Arab North Africa, the Fertile Crescent, and the Arabian Peninsula.[4] Many of the problems that the region is experiencing now have origins that stretch back a century, but the immediate crisis and wars began with the Arab uprisings of 2010–11.

As was the case with the Thirty Years War, abortive peace negotiations have accompanied much of Syria's seven-year civil war since 2011. Talks between the Syrian government, some opposition groups, regional powers, and the United States and Russia have been brokered by various institutions and states, beginning with the peace initiatives launched by the Arab League in late 2011. Further talks, sponsored by the UN and largely following a Western agenda, were conducted in Vienna and Geneva, while talks sponsored by Russia and focusing on reaching an accommodation with Turkey and Iran, and reflecting a more pro-Assad agenda, have taken place more recently in Astana and Sochi. The basic reason why these talks are not producing the desired results is that they are all too narrow in their scope (seeking the creation of limited peace zones), and not inclusive enough in terms of participants. The Geneva and Vienna talks largely failed to engage with the major pro-Assad powers, Russia and Iran, while the recent Astana and Sochi talks have largely failed to engage with the more stringent anti-Assad powers and groups. All sets of talks have failed to include certain key actors, including the Kurds and the Salafist Islamist groups, despite these being major belligerents in the conflict. More broadly, the resolution of the Syria conflict needs to be addressed within the context of a wider 'grand bargain' that seeks to address all interrelated conflicts that are raging across the Middle East now—this being a key lesson from the abortive, sectional peace initiatives that failed to end the Thirty Years War.

Three main interacting features and dynamics explain the outbreak and course of the current conflict: the crisis of legitimacy in the Middle East, sectarianism, and the Saudi–Iranian dualism as well as wider great power rivalry in the region. It only makes sense to separate these factors up to a point, because they often merge to produce certain outcomes (such as proxy wars and interventions resulting from a combination of the crisis of legitimacy leading to uprisings, and Iran and Saudi Arabia then feeling compelled by their rivalry to become involved in the unrest), or are virtually inseparable by the nature of their manifestation (such as the sectarian element of Saudi–Iranian antagonism, which cannot be explained merely in terms of geo-strategic realpolitik). Some phenomena, like jihadi terrorism, are fuelled by all three elements.

Crisis of legitimacy in the Middle East

The Arab world has been in the throes of a legitimacy crisis for around a century. The Arab states that emerged from the French and British mandates, which had resulted from the dismemberment of the Ottoman Empire after its defeat in the First World War, never enjoyed much of a sense of legitimacy among their subjects. They were viewed by many as by-products of Western imperial duplicity and manipulation. The Entente powers had in effect transported to the Middle East a system of sovereign nation-states which had existed in Europe from the nineteenth century (and which was already attributed to the legacy of the Peace of Westphalia). But the fit was not as good in the Middle East as it was in Europe (and it was arguably none too successful there either). Despite having revolted against the Ottoman Turks in support of the Entente powers, the Arabs did not receive a single large kingdom, but were instead given several small states, most of which were initially under French or British supervision.[5] These Arab republics largely turned out to be failures, to a greater or lesser extent. Even after they had shaken off colonial rule, they failed to deliver either material prosperity or their much-vaunted goals of Arab unity and the liberation of Palestine. They kept their populations in check through harsh dictatorial rule and state repression, while relying on external support from either the United States or the Soviet Union during the Cold War. The emergence of political Islam, particularly the transnational Muslim Brotherhood, personified by Sayyid Qutb, who was executed in 1966 by the dictatorial regime of Gamal Abdel Nasser in Egypt, was to an extent a reaction both against secular Arab autocracy and against the failure of Arab nationalism to achieve its aims.

Political Islam was one strand of societal opposition to the old order of repressive secular dictatorship. Another erupted spectacularly at the end of

2010 during the Arab Spring with a wave of popular protests and uprisings aimed at democratic reform, greater political freedoms, greater economic opportunities, and an end to corruption. Numerous long-term Arab dictators were deposed from power by their own people in 2011: Zine el-Abidine Ben Ali of Tunisia, Hosni Mubarak of Egypt, Muammar Qaddafi of Libya (with the help of a Western aerial military intervention), and Yemen's Ali Abdullah Saleh. The uprising in Syria against the regime of Bashar al-Assad was met with violent repression and has morphed into a bloody multi-sided civil war involving numerous direct and proxy interventions by regional and global powers. That conflict has merged with the Iraqi civil war from 2014, with a key element linking the two being the declaration of the Islamic State's extreme Islamist caliphate straddling the old Sykes-Picot border between the two states. The defeat of IS has not ended the fighting in Syria between the Assad regime and its enemies, and the tensions in Iraq could easily again flare up into serious conflict. The new internationally recognised government in Yemen has been driven out by long-standing regime opponents, the Houthi rebels, whose take-over in partnership with former President Saleh led to a devastating civil war which is now largely being directed from without the country. In Egypt, the revolution which led to the election of the Muslim Brotherhood-linked Mohamed Morsi in 2012 was suppressed by the army which launched a counter-revolutionary coup in 2013 and installed Abdel Fattah el-Sisi as dictator.

The Arab monarchies of the Gulf, though often just as devoid of political and societal freedoms as their republican counterparts, fared much better during the Arab Spring, although the rentier model economy is becoming increasingly unstable. Similarly, Spain was an early rentier state, its economy reliant on bullion from the Indies. In part the resilience of monarchical dynasties in the Gulf and elsewhere in the Middle East and North Africa has been due to their ability to pay off their subjects lavishly with petrodollars and natural gas revenues in order to stave off rebellion (there were no protests in Qatar and the UAE); in part it may be explained by a carefully crafted long-term image in which the ruling dynasty is equated with the state itself, and in some cases can claim traditional legitimacy by descent from the Prophet.[6] Another reason may be the greater propensity of a ruler who has comfortably inherited power to undertake steps to redress grievances, than a renegade who had been willing to risk his life by seizing power in a coup some decades prior and had viewed the state as his booty, to be passed on to a son.[7] It was precisely the perceived ambition of some of the republican dictators, such as those of

Egypt, Tunisia and Yemen, to establish their own dynasties, as had already occurred in Syria, which aroused extra resentment among their people.[8]

Apart from Tunisia, where a fragile democratic transition has taken hold, the legitimacy deficit remains throughout the Middle East. Similarly, the Thirty Years War can be described as the Empire's constitutional crisis,[9] which was at heart also a crisis of legitimacy. Of course, the values attached to legitimacy were of a different age, but similar questions regarding the lawfulness and validity of the basis of rule and the extent to which rights were respected or disregarded were at the forefront of the Dutch rebellion against the Spanish Habsburgs, the Bohemian rebellion against the Austrian Habsburgs, and the princes' rebellion against the Habsburgs as Emperors. The main reason why the hopes of the uprisings of 2010–12 have been scuppered is that the rebellions descended into sectarian conflict and led to the opening up of channels of interference into destabilised weak states, which drew in rival regional and global powers, particularly Iran and Saudi Arabia.

Saudi–Iranian dualism and great power rivalry

Great power competition, especially between the regional powers Saudi Arabia and Iran, but also between the global powers America and Russia, has greatly exacerbated the recent strife in the Middle East, through proxy wars and interventions in states destabilised and 'opened up' by the uprisings of the Arab Spring. Domestic unrest has often been caused by the factors mentioned above, but following the resulting collapse of states, the Saudi–Iran dualism attained greater importance.

Proxy conflict and interventionism are nothing new in the region. They have been central features of international politics in the Middle East for the last century or so, often played out in the context of the Cold War. In 1953 Britain and the United States initiated the overthrow of a democratic government in Iran in order to prevent oil nationalisation, strengthen the monarchy and safeguard its anti-communist alignment. Usually, however, interventions and the sponsorship of proxies occurred in smaller, peripheral states of the region, including Yemen and among rival Palestinian factions. Lebanon with its multitude of quarrelsome heterogeneous communities has been particularly susceptible to external interventions. Abortive American interventions took place there in 1958 and during the civil war in the 1980s. Syria also intervened in Lebanon during this conflict and remained the dominant external power broker in Lebanon until it was ejected in 2005.[10] What distinguishes the current round of interventionism and faction-sponsoring in the aftermath of the Arab Spring is the centrality to the regional system of the states affected, such as Syria and Egypt,[11] again mirroring the situation in the Thirty Years War where interventions were focused on the Holy Roman Empire at the heart of the European state system.

Following the collapse of the Soviet Union and the end of the Cold War, the United States cemented its position as the global hegemon, including in the Middle East. Its policies were aimed at maintaining the status quo, often in partnership with autocratic rulers of the region. Few resisted American leadership, but among those that did were Iran, Iraq and, to a lesser extent, Syria. Following the terrorist attacks by al-Qaeda against the heartland of the United States in 2001, American policy shifted towards a bolder and more ambitious approach of reordering the region along democratic lines, while drastically increasing the US military presence in the Middle East to flush out terrorists. Under the Presidency of George W. Bush one of the more vicious dictators of the region was removed and killed following the American-led invasion of Iraq in 2003, and the region's lone democracy, Israel, was given greater support, emboldening it to conduct a series of armed actions against Palestinian militants and Lebanese Hezbollah.

Under President Barack Obama, the Americans scaled back their commitments and presence in the Middle East and focused greater attention towards East Asia. US forces, which had reached a peak of over 170,000 troops in 2007, withdrew from Iraq in 2011. US support for Israel became less robust, and the guiding goal of American policy in the region became to secure an agreement with Iran to halt or delay its nuclear weapons programme in return for a reduction of sanctions, a goal that was achieved in 2015. This relative American disengagement set the stage for heightened tensions and rivalry between Saudi Arabia and Iran, coinciding with the popular Arab uprisings of 2011–12.

Traditionally, Saudi Arabia has always seen itself, and has been seen by others in the Muslim world, as the leading Islamic power, with its kings serving as custodians of the mosques in Mecca and Medina, the two holiest sites of Islam. In terms of its international influence and engagement it has over the last decades eclipsed the much more populous fellow Sunni state of Egypt. Saudi leadership has been challenged by the largest Shia state, Iran, after the revolution of 1979 established an Islamic republic there. Since the founding of the Islamic republic, Iran has viewed the United States as its greatest enemy, although it is also extremely hostile towards Israel, denying its right to exist.

Saudi Arabia is a long-standing ally of the United States. Iran's essentially defensive posture developed as a result of the long and immensely destructive Iraq–Iran war (1980–8), which broke out as a result of a full-scale invasion by Saddam Hussein.

Despite the long-term enmity between Iran and the US, the American toppling of Saddam Hussein and the subsequent state collapse in Iraq greatly benefited Iran as its most aggressive opponent in the Arab world was removed. Although Iran, did not welcome the large-scale introduction of American forces along its western border in Iraq, as well as along its eastern border in Afghanistan, it was able to take advantage of the subsequent turmoil in Iraq. The new Shia-dominated government under Nouri al-Maliki elected by the Iraq's Shia majority population was friendly towards Iran (although it was also propped up by the Americans), and Iran has been able to extend its influence into the country through its support of Shia militias.[12]

The sudden eruption of the Arab uprisings across the region in 2011 presented both opportunities and threats to the two regional powers, Saudi Arabia and Iran, whose rivalry for regional influence has been geared up considerably in the context of the region-wide unrest. This is because supporting uprisings and rebellions against governments aligned with either Iran or Saudi Arabia presents a great opportunity to the other, which then felt obliged to stand by its allied government in order to ensure its survival and thereby shut out the regional rival's influence as far as possible. Therefore, in the highly charged context of a cold war between two large powers on either side of weaker states, insurrection and instability in the latter almost compels outside involvement and intervention. Thus, Saudi Arabia has supported and sponsored rebels fighting the Iran-backed Syrian government, while helping the governments of Yemen and Bahrain to fight uprisings, mainly by Shias believed to be backed by Iran. A similar dynamic underpinned the interventions in the Thirty Years War in Europe. Iran's priorities are Syria, Iraq and Lebanon, where it supports allies and proxies, but it has given at least moral support to anti-Saudi elements elsewhere, in Bahrain and Qatar, and more than that in Yemen, after Saudi attacks forced the Houthis to seek their help.

The year 2015 marked an escalation of the regional conflict and the Iran–Saudi cold war. The conclusion of the Iran nuclear deal, in which the five permanent members of the UN Security Council plus Germany and the European Union came to an agreement with Iran following talks in Vienna, was strongly opposed by Saudi Arabia and the other Sunni Gulf monarchies, as well as by Israel. They feared that the deal marked the beginning of a more conciliatory stance towards Iran by the United States, an apprehension which encouraged Saudi Arabia to take the initiative in aggressively containing Iran during a period in which US efforts were seen as half-hearted.[13] Thus, the Saudis launched a large-scale military intervention in Yemen that same year, supported by their Sunni allies, the United Arab Emirates, Bahrain, Egypt and Jordan, among others. The United States and Britain have provided limited assistance and arms sales. The Saudi-led coalition targeted the Shia Houthi rebels, who have been given some support by Iran, backing the internationally recognised government of Abdrabbuh Mansur Hadi. In 2015 the Iranian-backed government of Assad in Syria also received the decisive support of Russia, which intervened by launching often indiscriminate air strikes against the anti-regime rebels, including those supported by Saudi Arabia and the United States, as well as against Islamic State terrorists.

The Syrian civil war rapidly became an ever-riskier geopolitical flashpoint, sucking in an increasing number of external powers. With the Iranian Revolutionary Guards' Quds Forces and their Lebanese Hezbollah clients already on the ground fighting in defence of Assad, who was being supported from the air by Russian forces, the Saudis, Americans and other allied and Western countries were backing and funding the same rebels that the Russians and Iranians were fighting. The potential for the various patrons backing opposing sides to come into direct conflict with each other was made dramatically clear in November 2015 when Turkey, which had been supporting the anti-Assad forces, shot down a Russian fighter jet. If Syria and other Middle Eastern flashpoints were neutralised and taken out of ongoing geopolitical rivalry, as the Holy Roman Empire was after Westphalia in 1648, it would reduce the risk of direct state-on-state war among the major powers, in addition to ending the terrible death toll and human suffering on the ground.

While often on the defensive against American hostility, Iran has been emboldened by its perception of Arab weakness: the Arab states failed to drive Israel into the sea in the 1940s–1970s, they failed to defend Lebanon against Israel in the 1980s, and they failed to defend Kuwait in the 1990s, instead calling in the Americans. More recently, over the course of 2017 it increasingly appeared that Iran was winning the regional contest with Saudi Arabia. The mortal threat posed to the Assad regime by the Saudi-backed rebels had been neutralised, and Iran (together with Russia) came close to achieving a comprehensive victory in Syria. Iran's influence remains strong in the Shia-controlled Iraqi government and among militias there. Iran's ally Hezbollah dominates Lebanon. Some in the West have suggested that this brings the Iranians close to securing a land corridor stretching from Iran along the Fertile Crescent towards Lebanon and the Mediterranean Sea—perhaps reminiscent of the 'Spanish Road' between northern Italy and the Netherlands which the Habsburgs controlled in the late sixteenth and early seventeenth centuries. A senior adviser to the Iranian supreme leader, Ayatollah Khamenei, recently announced during a visit to Aleppo in Syria that 'the resistance line starts from Tehran and passes through Baghdad, Damascus and Beirut to reach Palestine'.[14] The Saudis feel threatened by this corridor as well as by the Iranian backing and supplying of the Houthi rebels in their southern backyard. The Israelis feel similarly threatened and have recently taken strong military action along their Syrian border, especially at the Golan Heights, to show that they will not accept an Iranian presence there. The Saudi intervention in Yemen has not been successful despite their bombing campaign inflicting massive casualties, and their blockade of western Yemen starving and exposing millions to disease.[15] After Saudi Arabia intercepted a ballistic missile—fired by the Houthi rebels and probably supplied by Iran—over Riyadh, the kingdom declared that it considered this an act of war by Iran. Saudi Arabia has levelled similar accusations against Hezbollah. The hitherto mainly proxy-driven conflicts between the two power blocs—Saudi Arabia, UAE, Bahrain and Israel on the one side, and Iran, Hezbollah and Shia militias in Iraq and Syria on the other side—appear to be coming close to a direct war.[16]

While the Saudis were largely on the defensive until early 2017, they have since then, under the de facto leadership of Crown Prince Muhammad bin Salman, become emboldened by the vociferous support of the United States under President Trump.[17] Donald Trump has also stated that he views Iran as one of the biggest state sponsors of terrorism, and has expressed a willingness to scrap the Iran nuclear deal because of its alleged leniency towards Tehran, a view shared by Saudi Arabia and Israel.[18] In fact, the latter two countries now find themselves in an unspoken state of quasi-alignment, as they both share hostility towards and fear of Iran and Hezbollah, and are both beneficiaries of strong—or at least vocal—US support under President Trump.[19] At the same time as consolidating his power grab inside the kingdom by sweeping aside carefully calibrated traditions of power-sharing and favour-trading during an extensive anti-corruption purge,[20] Muhammad bin Salman apparently turned his attention towards Lebanon as a possible new site of confrontation with Iran after the failure of Saudi efforts in Yemen.[21] By summoning the Saudi-aligned Lebanese prime minister Saad Hariri to Riyadh and seemingly forcing him to resign (a move paralleled by the Spanish forces' arrest of the elector of

Trier for being too close to the French in 1635), Prince Muhammad might have intended to expose the Lebanese government as being under the control of Hezbollah and therefore, by proxy, Iran, in order to better justify sanctions or more forceful measures—but his heavy-handed action again backfired.[22]

President Trump also expressed support for the Saudi-led blockade of Qatar in 2017 (though other voices from his administration have been more guarded). This event highlights another problem facing the Saudis in their confrontation with Iran: their inability to control and dominate a united Sunni front against Tehran.[23] The Gulf Cooperation Council (GCC) has long been ineffective as a political organisation, and there have been deep divisions between its members, despite most sharing a suspicion of Iran.[24] The UAE, Kuwait and Bahrain have largely toed the Saudi line against Iran. The Sunni ruling family of Bahrain is particularly indebted to the Saudis, after Riyadh launched an intervention in 2011 to support the King of Bahrain's violent suppression of large-scale anti-government protests by the Shia majority population. Fabulously wealthy but tiny, Qatar has refused to follow Saudi leadership in many areas, and has actively challenged the kingdom and its close Emirati allies. Uniquely among Gulf states, Qatar supported the initial Arab Spring uprisings. It has also been favourably disposed towards the Muslim Brotherhood and less moderate Islamist groups such as Hamas (which Iran has intermittently supported as well). Qatar often funded different groups and militias that were in rivalry with those supported by the Saudis or the UAE. The post-Gaddafi conflicts and developments in Libya were structured more by a rivalry between Qatar and the UAE than between Saudi Arabia and Iran.[25] Qatar's positioning of itself between the two main power blocs is comparable to a similar effort by a group of Protestant princes to establish themselves as a third party between Sweden and the Emperor at the 1631 colloquy of Leipzig.[26]

The role of Turkey, another major regional power and NATO member, complicates further the simple picture of a straightforward Saudi–Iranian dualism. As a (secular) Sunni power, it has long maintained cordial relations with Saudi Arabia, which is closely aligned with the leading NATO powers. Like Saudi Arabia, Turkey has also strongly opposed the Assad regime in Syria and has supported rebels fighting the government. Yet Turkey also shares an interest with Iran in preventing the establishment of a Kurdish state out of a fear that this will strengthen Kurdish irredentism and energise the Turkish Kurds of the Kurdistan Workers' Party (PKK), the defeat of whose separatist ambitions is a vital Turkish interest. Turkey's military intervention in northern

Syria in 2016–17, 'Operation Euphrates Shield', was primarily designed to push back Syrian fighters of the Kurdish People's Protection Units (YPG), which have themselves been backed by the Americans. Turkish President Erdoğan has steered a middle course between Saudi Arabia and Iran at the regional level, and between the United States and Russia at the global level. In recent times he has moved further away from the US position, for example expressing consternation at the Americans' support for the predominantly Kurdish Syrian Democratic Forces (SDF), and attacking them during their second major military intervention in northern Syria in January 2018, entitled, with miserable irony, 'Operation Olive Branch'. This intervention received tacit approval from Russia and risked putting a great strain on relations with the United States. But the geopolitical encirclement of Turkey by Russia—to the north across the Black Sea, to the east in the former Soviet republics which are in Russia's orbit of influence, and to the south in Syria—is also likely to be perceived as a security threat by Ankara.[27] In the conflict between Qatar and Saudi Arabia, Turkey came down decisively in support of Qatar, where it has a military base, emboldening Qatari resistance against Saudi bullying, and again distancing itself from Trump's position.[28] Furthermore, Erdoğan no longer insists that Assad would need to be removed from power in a future peace settlement, thereby shifting further towards the Iranian–Russian stance.[29]

In fact, that triad (Turkey, Iran, Russia) has been the driving force behind the latest peace negotiations in the Syrian conflict. The UN-sponsored and US-dominated talks in Geneva, which had aimed to set out a future constitution for Syria, have failed to make substantive progress. In a reflection of the growing ascendancy of Russia (and Iran) in the Syria conflict, the diplomatic focus of the peace process has shifted towards the Russian-sponsored talks in Astana over the course of 2017, which also gained the support of the US special envoy for Syria, Staffan de Mistura. The leading negotiating powers, Russia, Iran and Turkey, agreed on the establishment of four 'de-escalation zones' which are designed to reduce conflict between Syrian government forces and the Turkish-supported rebels. The three powers in question also agreed to serve as guarantors of these de-escalation zones.[30] The latest round of peace talks was also sponsored by the Russians, at Sochi, which included a great number of Syrian delegates, although these were largely pro-Assad.[31] The peace talks dominated by Russia, Iran and Turkey at Astana and Sochi now seem much more likely to make progress than the Western-sponsored Geneva talks, with a consequent shift away from an emphasis on the necessity of removing Assad from power, towards a willingness to countenance his continued rule, albeit under external supervision.[32] One possible reason for the shifting diplomatic balance towards the Eastern powers is President Trump's seeming lack of interest in reaching a settlement in the Middle East, beyond destroying the Islamic State and giving Saudi Arabia strong rhetorical support against Iran (one strike against a Syrian regime airfield in response to a chemical weapons massacre of civilians in April 2017 notwithstanding).

The ways in which the existing dynamics of great power rivalry interacted with instances of local unrest and rebellion, to produce an internationalisation of conflict through the exporting of instability and the importing of intervention, are comparable to the incremental escalation of conflict during the Thirty Years War. The hostility and competition between Iran and Saudi Arabia are comparable to the rivalry between the Habsburgs (Spain and Austria) and France. One factor which distinguishes the current conflict between Iran and Saudi Arabia, however, is the role of sectarianism, which in the Middle Eastern scenario is reinforced by great power competition.

Sectarianism

As a driver of conflict and instability, sectarianism is linked to the issue of legitimacy in the sense that the religious schism between Sunni and Shia—almost as old as Islam itself—is related less to theological differences than to the question of who was the legitimate political successor to the Prophet. For many centuries the Shia–Sunni divide was not marked by violence and hostility. In the more immediate context, Sunnis' resentment against Shias has combined with a legitimacy deficit in several states. In Syria, the tyrannical regime of Assad relied on a tight-knit network of support by his own Alawite sect (a branch of Shia Islam) as well as other minorities, while excluding the Sunni majority from favour and participation. This minority rule was aided by a hostile sectarian narrative.[33] Iraq's Sunnis, albeit in a minority, felt similarly excluded under the partisan Shia government of Nouri al-Maliki. In Lebanon, non-Shia groups are under the yoke of the powerful Hezbollah, and in Yemen the Zaydi Houthi rebels seized control of much of the country, precipitating the devastating civil war.

The Arab Spring, which initially appeared driven not by such 'backward' sentiments as sectarian antagonism, but by more progressive aspirations such as democratisation, has descended into sectarianised conflict in many quarters. In Syria, Assad's Alawite forces are backed by Shia Hezbollah fighters, Iranian

Revolutionary Guards and Shia volunteers from across the region, and are fighting against Sunni rebels supported by Saudi Arabia and other Sunni states, and against the radical Sunni Islamic State.[34]

Before the outbreak of the Arab Spring, Iraq had already witnessed a wave of sectarian violence in the mid-2000s, amounting in essence to a sectarian civil war. Al-Qaeda fighters in Iraq were driven as much by hatred of Shias as by their opposition to the Americans' presence. Sunni governments around this time also expressed great suspicion of Shia powers' ambitions in highly sectarian language, such as King Abdullah of Jordan warning against the encroaching spectre of a hostile 'Shia crescent' in 2004.[35] Sunni resentment against the pro-Shia partisanship of the al-Maliki government in Baghdad—justified according to the rule of the majority, in a way that is similar to the Catholics' marginalisation of Protestants by majority voting in the Imperial Diet during the late sixteenth century and early seventeenth century[36]—was an important reason for the rise of Islamic State in Iraq and the subsequent merging of the Syrian and Iraqi civil wars in 2014.

The cold war between Iran and Saudi Arabia is driven by a combination of geopolitical competition and sectarian animosity. Sectarian tensions between the two countries intensified when Saudi Arabia executed the prominent Saudi Shia cleric, Nimr al-Nimr, in January 2016. While Iran's anger at this killing was genuine enough, both powers have also actively and artificially encouraged a 'confessionalisation' of conflicts and rivalries, to an extent that was absent in the great power rivalry between France and the Habsburgs because both were Catholic. Actively encouraging sectarianism has had both domestic and foreign political purposes. In response to the Iranian revolution of 1979 and the occupation of the Grand Mosque in Mecca by Sunni fundamentalists in the same year, the Saudi government attempted to co-opt, appease and embrace radical Wahhabi Islam by funding the exportation of its values across the globe and ostensibly rejecting Western models at home.[37] The Saudis have been able to justify repressing their Shia subjects in the east of the kingdom by fostering sectarianism and portraying them as a potential Iranian fifth column. In terms of regional politics, provoking sectarian sentiment served the Saudi purpose of undermining the appeal of Iran's intense hostility towards Israel and the United States among Arabs across the region.[38]

In general, authoritarian regimes have been able to undermine domestic calls for reform by dismissing them as sectarian rebellions controlled by outside powers. Sunni Gulf regimes largely invented the spectre of an Iranian-controlled 'Shi'ite threat' in their midst, with the aim of driving a wedge between their subjects, and enlisting unconditional support for the dynasty among Sunnis. This power-political strategy aimed at power retention was used by the Bahraini and Saudi governments to suppress protests in Bahrain and eastern Saudi Arabia in 2011, for example.[39] The sectarian narrative peddled by the Gulf governments risked becoming a self-fulfilling prophecy, however, as Iran has indeed reached out to Shia communities, who in turn might be more receptive to such overtures as a result of the discrimination they suffer from the government-sponsored injection of sectarianism.[40] The accusation of being a fifth column, simply a tool for Iranian interests, is therefore potentially damaging and has led Shia militia groups in Iraq, Yemen and elsewhere to be highly sensitive about this image.[41]

While the fault lines of conflict in the Middle East broadly correspond to confessional divisions, it would be inaccurate to conceive of the conflict as a simple, region-wide Sunni vs Shia religious war, just as the Thirty Years War cannot be conceived simply as a confessional war between Catholics and Protestants. Divisions within the 'Sunni camp', particularly between Saudi Arabia and Qatar, have sometimes been almost as important in driving conflict.[42] Furthermore, although the oil-rich Sunni monarchies of the Gulf have infused the Arab Spring and regional conflicts with sectarian hate speech, and have sponsored Sunni rebel groups, their relationship with Sunni Islamism is far from straightforward. They are hostile towards the radical Sunni terror groups, who in turn view the Gulf monarchies as decadent and pro-Western. Several Gulf states (not Qatar) also supported the military coup against the more moderate Islamist and democratically elected government of the Muslim Brotherhood in Egypt, precisely because the Brotherhood represented an alternative, more democratic model of Sunni Islamic government, which could threaten the legitimacy of Gulf absolutist monarchical rule.[43] Conversely, it would also be misguided and reductive to view sectarian sentiment as a mere fig leaf for hegemonic aggrandisement in a realpolitik-driven conflict between great powers. Many Western academics and commentators suffer from a conceptual myopia towards the continued importance of religion, both in contemporary international politics and in post-1648 Europe. In fact it often lies at the heart of paranoia and the exaggeration and miscalculation of opponents' motives and steps.[44]

PART II

HISTORIES

3

FROM RELIGIOUS PEACE TO THE THIRTY YEARS WAR

MULTIPLE CRISES IN EUROPE AND THE HOLY ROMAN EMPIRE, 1555–1648

In previous years ... inhabitants of the kingdom have faced, suffered, and endured many and various kinds of terrible hardships and tribulations in both political and ecclesiastical affairs ... Thereby they evilly plagued the subjects in diverse ways on account of religion, had them banished under the pretence of secular malfeasances ... and used unheard-of atrocities to force people to convert to the Catholic religion against their will and against the clear language of the Letter of Majesty.

Apologia of the Bohemian noble territorial estates, justifying the defenestration of Prague, 25 May 1618[1]

Once the most serene king of Sweden considered ... the bonds of honour, proximity, common religion, liberty and commerce, ... His Royal Majesty could then not wait any longer to come to the assistance of the oppressed, who had so urgently requested help, solace, and advice; nor to act for the benefit of neighbours and friends, and also for both his own and the public and common security.

King Gustavus Adolphus of Sweden, Manifesto justifying the intervention against the Emperor in Germany, July 1630[2]

The Thirty Years War was a highly complex conflict which spread from a local rebellion in Bohemia, one of the constituent territories of the Empire, to the Holy Roman Empire as a whole, thus becoming an Imperial civil war, before finally attracting outside intervention from among the neighbouring European great powers. There was an incremental escalation or internationalisation of the war, whereby a local rebellion turned into a general civil war and then merged with ongoing great power rivalries and conflicts. The two opening epigraphs of this chapter are quotations from key decision-makers justifying their actions at successive stages of conflict escalation: the Bohemian rebels explaining the reasons for their actions (at which stage the rebellion began and then became an Imperial civil war), and the justification of one of the major external interventions in the Imperial civil war, which marked an important stage in its European escalation. In order to explain the causes of the war, as well as the factors which explain why it was able to escalate incrementally, it is necessary to explain the origins of tensions and conflict constellations at three basic layers or levels: the local (Bohemia and the Habsburg hereditary lands), the 'regional' (the Holy Roman Empire), and the international (Europe).[3]

European great power rivalries and conflicts in the sixteenth and early seventeenth century

The internal crisis within the Holy Roman Empire became Europeanised very soon after the outbreak of the war in 1618, with Spain giving support to the Emperor and the Dutch providing limited support to the rebels, before European powers became the main belligerents from the 1630s. It is therefore necessary to understand the great power rivalries, divisions and conflicts which form the backdrop to the internationalisation of the war.[4]

During the first half of the sixteenth century, the international system was centred predominantly around the Franco-Habsburg dualism. While this rivalry persisted in the second half of the sixteenth century and in the seventeenth century, the international system in the decades leading up to the Thirty Years War was increasingly in flux on account of its growing pluralisation.[5] Several of the wars of the period have been interpreted by historians as state-building wars resulting from an attempt by individual component entities of larger conglomerates of states, which shared the same monarch in personal union, to break away and assert their independence from these 'composite monarchies'[6] that dominated Europe.[7] Although the international system had not yet been widely conceptualised as an integrated whole, European statesmen and diplomats were already aware of the interconnected nature of the various regional balances, or sub-systems, as seen for example in the practice of 'leapfrog diplomacy', whereby one power would entice a distant state to put pressure on a more proximate rival from the rear, in order to improve its own geopolitical position in its own region of interest.[8]

The reason for the importance of this international context of the broader European arena, and also a reason for the rapid drawing in of European powers into the Imperial civil war, is the centrality of the Holy Roman Empire to the European international system. Located at the geopolitical heart of Europe, Germany was the pivot of the European inter-state system, and it was here that the interests of all the major European powers, including France, Spain, the Netherlands, Denmark, Sweden, and even England and Turkey, intersected. This was not just a question of geography. As a decentralised polity with a multitude of power centres, the Empire was incapable of harnessing its vast resources behind a unified programme of power projection and expansion. Preventing the decentralised Empire from falling under the domination of a rival power within or without Germany was a vital security interest for European powers, and one that many states were willing to go to war for, as they did during the Thirty Years War. The central position and manpower resources of the Empire were such that it could not be ignored by outside powers—just as the natural gas and oil-rich Middle East cannot be disregarded by external powers now. Its polycentric nature gave its numerous neighbours manifold opportunities to establish links and networks of patronage, sponsorship and protection with local princes or groups of princes. This, along with the princes' own jealous guarding of their liberties and privileges, helped to ensure the continuation of the Empire's decentralised constitutional set-up. The web of European–Imperial interconnections was strengthened by the numerous dynastic links between German and European princely and royal families. Almost all European international problems and crises at the time therefore also had a German dimension.[9]

The European wars and crises on the periphery of the Empire do not explain why the Thirty Years War occurred—it had its own causes as a distinct conflict in Germany—but understanding them is important in explaining why the Imperial civil war in Germany became intertwined with European great power conflicts early on, by becoming internationalised through external intervention.

The competition between France and the Habsburg powers was the dominant rivalry, between the most powerful state actors, in European geopolitics in the early modern period. It is the equivalent of the Saudi–Iranian rivalry in the Middle East, the chief difference being that France and the Habsburgs were not divided by religion (they were both Catholic), and that they often engaged in direct full-scale war. France had a large population, was territorially compact, and possessed a centralised constitutional system with a powerful army, but was temporarily weakened internally by religious wars until the end of the 1620s. The Habsburgs possessed more territory, but it was more fragmented. Following the reign of Emperor Charles V, the Habsburg 'universal empire' was divided into an Austrian and a Spanish branch. The Austrian Habsburgs possessed the largest single-dynasty conglomeration of territories in the Empire, the so-called hereditary lands of Bohemia and Austria. The Habsburg candidate had always been elected Emperor since the mid-fifteenth century. In addition to the Spanish kingdoms of Castile and Aragon, the Spanish Habsburgs possessed Portugal from 1580, Naples and Sicily, parts of northern Italy, Franche-Comté, and the Netherlands. Appended to the crowns of Spain and Portugal were vast colonial empires in the Americas that furnished valuable supplies of silver. France considered Spain to be the more formidable enemy. French armies and diplomacy supported rebellions against Spanish rule at various times in the Netherlands, Catalonia, Naples and Portugal, and supported states that were hostile to Spain in Italy (primarily the Venetian Republic). France also had a long tradition of setting up patronage networks and relationships of protection of clients within the Empire that were directed against the Habsburg Emperor. Spain in turn also intervened in France's domestic affairs, such as by providing assistance to enemies of the crown during the French wars of religion. In 1617, the two branches of the Habsburgs concluded an alliance which facilitated rapid Spanish intervention in support of the Austrian Habsburg Emperor soon after the outbreak of war the following year. Spain's support of its Austrian cousins was largely aimed at securing the Spanish Road supplying their theatre of war in the Low Countries, but the family and religious ties were also still significant.[10]

This war in the Netherlands began as a rebellion of the Protestant northern provinces against Spanish rule in 1566, but by the turn of the century they had established themselves as a de facto independent power, the Republic of the United Netherlands, while the largely Catholic southern Netherlands (present-day Belgium) remained under Spanish rule. The Dutch Republic possessed great trading wealth and its continued war against Spain was highly costly for Spain, because of the loss to Spanish shipping which the powerful Dutch navy was able to inflict, and not least because of the logistical difficulties in supplying the Spanish armies fighting in the Low Countries. For this purpose, the so-called Spanish Road was vitally important. It was a land corridor stretching from Italy to the Netherlands; a Spanish military supply route connected across a patchwork of Habsburg territories.[11] Keeping the Spanish Road open was an important geopolitical consideration in Madrid's decision to enter the war in support of the Austrian Habsburgs.[12]

Another theatre of conflict whose actors were liable to be drawn into a war in the Holy Roman Empire was that of the Baltic Sea in northern Europe. The Empire had a long Baltic coastline, and one of the leading powers, Denmark, held territory in the Empire and was therefore an Imperial Estate in its own right. The two main sets of rivalries here were between Sweden and Denmark, and between Sweden and Poland, the latter two countries being in an almost perpetual state of war or cold war until the 1660s.[13]

In south-west Europe, there was a perennial risk of an attack on the Habsburgs, and other Christian powers, by the Ottoman Turks. But while the above-mentioned sets of conflicts and rivalries tended to divide the members of the Empire, the Turkish threat from the Balkans had a unifying effect. Viewed as the 'hereditary enemy of Christendom', the Sultan's aggression against the Empire served as a cross-confessional unifying bracket, especially during the Long Turkish War of 1593–1606.[14] The conclusion of a peace treaty between the Emperor and the Turks in 1606 caused this solidarity effect to fade, allowing internal political tensions and confessional and constitutional conflicts within the Empire to come to the fore, in a manner that is perhaps comparable to the reduced potency of shared hostility towards Israel in the early twenty-first century—allowing tensions and divisions among Arabs and Muslims in the Middle East to grow to greater prominence.

Confessional tensions and political paralysis in the Holy Roman Empire[15]

Whereas the sectarian element of the contemporary strife in the Middle East derives from a religious schism that originated well over a millennium earlier, the Thirty Years War broke out in Europe a mere century after the schism of western Christianity. The Protestant Reformation, which began in 1517, posed a great challenge for the newly rearranged Imperial constitution and its institutions. The challenge derived in part from the absence of a modern separation of church from state in the Empire. The Empire was 'holy' in the sense that it was founded as a result of an agreement between the first emperor, Charlemagne, and the Papacy, and the popes continued to crown emperors until the sixteenth century.[16] The Emperor retained a religious duty to defend Christianity and the church, and numerous Imperial Estates were ecclesiastical territories, in which temporal political rule was carried out by a bishop, archbishop or a prelate. In such territories political and spiritual authority elided. The Reformation's challenge also derived from the fact that it attracted ruling princes (most importantly Saxony, Brandenburg, the Palatinate, Hessen-Kassel, Hanover and most Imperial cities), not just subjects, as had been the case with previous heresies, which could be suppressed more easily. Secular princes were attracted to Protestantism by the prospect of secularising (i.e. confiscating) valuable Catholic church property within their territories, and by asserting emergency spiritual authority themselves, thereby extending the remit of their rule over their subjects considerably through intensified state-building. Ruling city councils of Imperial cities realised that adopting the Reformation helped to foster communal unity and autonomy, especially as many of their citizens had taken up the new faith themselves.

Emperor Charles V proscribed the initiator of the Reformation, Martin Luther, by placing him under the so-called 'Imperial ban', and also banned his writings, but this could not constrain the growing appeal of Protestantism, among both inhabitants and princes. After a series of relatively limited wars in the 1540s and 1550s the ruling princes and the Emperor's court came to the recognition that the religious schism could not be solved theologically or militarily. At the Imperial Diet of Augsburg, they therefore moved towards accepting confessional coexistence as a measure of last resort and sought to regulate it legally. The resulting Religious Peace of Augsburg (1555) was a working compromise on the religious question, which was achieved by shelving intractable questions of theological truth for the time being. It was a milestone in the development of confessional cohabitation, because it embodied, for the first time, a recognition of the importance of creating a legal-political framework to manage religious coexistence. It was the first time that the divinely ordained order of a unity of spiritual and secular law was disrupted, because it entailed the unprecedented divergence between the religious and the political order.[17]

With the Augsburg settlement, the ban on Lutheran Protestantism was lifted and Protestants were granted equal status to Catholics. The protection of the Eternal Territorial Peace (which had been proclaimed in 1495) was henceforth extended to Lutheran rulers. Religiously motivated military aggression was now also banned (as indeed was the use of force in general). The princes were granted the right to choose between the Catholic and the Lutheran faith and were entitled to impose their religion onto their territories, the Right of Reformation (*ius reformandi*). It was agreed that all secularised property formerly belonging to the Catholic Church that had been confiscated before 1552 could remain so after 1555.[18]

This was a good working solution, which brought peace for many decades. From the mid-1550s until the mid-1570s the Imperial institutions, based on consensus, compromise and cooperation, functioned very smoothly. But it was nevertheless structurally deficient and left several issues unresolved, which increasingly caused tension from the late 1570s. First, the Augsburg peace only granted Lutheran rulers protection under the Territorial Peace, while the other major branch of Protestantism, Reformed Calvinism and other sects remained banned and were officially heresies. Secondly, the princes only granted each other toleration between themselves, not among subjects within their territories. The Right of Reformation meant that subjects could be forced to convert to the religion which their prince had chosen (either Catholicism or Lutheranism). This was a form of religious compulsion later encapsulated in the phrase *cuius regio eius religio* ('the religion of the prince is the religion of the territory'). This was a state-centric solution—it ignored the concerns of the princes' subjects, apart from guaranteeing their right to emigrate (*ius emigrandi*—no small achievement, though, as this was the first basic individual right granted to most German subjects). Partially designed to undercut interventionist impulses by consigning confessional affairs to an inviolable domestic sphere, the treaty text stated: 'No Estate [territory] should protect and shield another Estate or its subjects against their government in any way.'[19]

But even from a state-centric perspective, it was increasingly unsatisfactory for Protestant territorial states, because—thirdly—the ecclesiastical territories were excluded from the Right of Reformation and their Catholic status was thereby fixed. This 'Ecclesiastical Reservation' put ecclesiastical princes who converted to Protestantism in a legally precarious position, because they were required to abdicate if they became Protestant. This issue of Protestant 'administrators' of ecclesiastical territories (as they were known after converting to Protestantism) being refused representation in the Imperial Diet or refusing to abdicate caused several crises and minor military confrontations in the 1580s, for example when the Protestant administrator of the archbishop-electorate of Cologne was deposed by the Pope and then driven out of the territory by an alliance of Catholic princes after refusing to vacate the electoral Cologne government. The brother of the Emperor, Ferdinand, who had negotiated the Augsburg Peace with the Protestant Imperial Estates, had issued an informal declaration in 1555, which was, however, not entered into the treaty. It stipulated that Protestant nobles living in ecclesiastical territories could remain Lutheran. From the late sixteenth century this was increasingly disregarded by Catholic rulers, who questioned its validity.[20]

Fourthly, the Ecclesiastical Reservation helped ensure an inbuilt Catholic majority in consultative and legislative assemblies, primarily the Imperial Diet, but also in the diets of the various circles (districts). The increasing willingness of the Catholic Imperial Estates to resort to majority voting, thereby marginalising Protestants and overruling their concerns, led to a fundamental paralysis of the Imperial constitution and its institutions, precisely because the smooth functioning of the system depended upon negotiated consensus, cooperation and compromise, which could not be achieved by an absolute reliance upon majorities. After the Catholics again used their majority to outvote the Protestants on religious matters at the Imperial Diet of 1613, and the Protestants in turn refused to accept the validity of its resolutions, no further Diet was convened until 1640. This question of absolute majority rule was a key factor in the crisis of the Empire before the Thirty Years War, which, although related to religious matters, was at heart a political and constitutional crisis. There are clear parallels here with the situation in Iraq under Nouri al-Maliki's narrow Shi'ite agenda, which was justified by the principle of majority rule but, by failing to include Sunnis, sowed the seeds for later strife and resistance against a tyranny of the majority. The Catholic domination of the legislature at the Imperial Diet had a knock-on effect on the functioning of the Imperial judiciary, which was also paralysed and seen as biased by Protestants. In sum, the ability to overcome sectarian tensions within the existing political-legal framework of the Imperial institutions, predicated upon consensus and compromise, increasingly proved to be illusory.[21]

There were other factors which also contributed to increasing tensions and paralysis from the mid-1570s. A new generation of more belligerent princes who had no personal memory of unity (such as the Emperors Matthias and Ferdinand II, Duke Maximilian of Bavaria, and the Elector Palatine Frederick V) began to replace the previous generation of consensus-oriented rulers who did have personal memory of the time of unity, such as Emperors Ferdinand I and Maximilian II. This generational change resulted in a reduced willingness to cooperate and compromise across confessional lines. Another cause of tensions was the assertiveness of the Tridentine Catholic reform movement and Counter-Reformation, a programme designed to roll back the effects of the Protestant Reformation which had been embarked upon as a result of decisions taken at a long-term crisis meeting of the Catholic Church in Trent between the 1540s and 1560s. The Counter-Reformation was driven by clerics and new orders such as Jesuits, and supported by Catholic princes.[22]

The rise of Calvinism from the 1560s severely destabilised the existing balance, especially because new recruits of the banned faith included a handful of leading princes such as the electors of the Palatine and of Brandenburg, and the landgrave of Hessen-Kassel. This caused a serious intra-Protestant fissure, as the new recruits usually converted from Lutheranism, whose members, such as the electors of Saxony, were more oriented to the status quo, loyal to the Emperor, and willing to cooperate with the Catholics in Imperial politics, because their position had largely been secured at Augsburg. The Calvinists, on the other hand, became more radical, and were determined to confessionalise disputes and thereby paralyse the system, precisely because the existing system did not accept their faith and put them in a legally precarious position. This heightened their willingness to disrupt and overturn existing arrangements. The Elector Palatine Frederick V was especially intent upon scaremongering, spreading fears of Catholic conspiracies and plots. As a result of this desire on the part of Catholic princes supporting the Counter-Reformation and of more radical, largely Calvinist Protestants to create a climate of confessional polarisation, conflicts that were not originally sectarian in nature become confessionalised and risked drawing in princes who were not originally affected. An example of this is the crisis over Jülich-Kleve in 1609–14, which was originally not related to religion at all—it was a succession dispute. But the contenders for the succession converted to different religions (to Calvinism and to Catholicism), partly in order to secure backing from their own religious camp.[23] In the Middle East, too, increasing sectarian polarisation has led conflicts that were originally tribal in nature, such as in Yemen, to become overlain by a dangerous sectarian dynamic. The Jülich-Kleve succession crisis also highlights the extent to which German dynastic and confessional politics were intertwined with European politics, as there was a real risk that this local conflict would lead to a general European war.[24]

To this institutional-political paralysis, one can add the general gloomy atmosphere that prevailed in central Europe around the turn of the century. Related to the Little Ice Age, there were social conflicts including peasants' rebellions, economic crisis, and the persecution of suspected witches in an age of uncertainty.[25] This general crisis atmosphere did not make war inevitable—the war was triggered by events within the Emperor's Habsburg hereditary lands. But it does help to explain why a local war within the Habsburg territories could spread quite rapidly to cover the rest of the Empire and become an Imperial civil war soon after the Bohemian rebellion. In short, the preceding has explained the preconditions for a rapid escalation of the conflict at the level of the Empire, not the causes of the war per se.

Crisis within the Habsburg dynasty and Bohemia: outbreak of the war

Problems within the Habsburg dynasty, especially the personal incapacity of Emperor Rudolf II (r. 1576–1612), also contributed to the failure to overcome sectarian tension and political crisis in the Empire. These internal Habsburg problems led to an inability of the Imperial dynasty to effectively manage the Empire, because the Emperor was unable or unwilling to act as a neutral broker and mediator. After all, every Imperial Estate, even radical Calvinist princes, accepted the role of the Emperor as the head of the Imperial hierarchy. This failure of the Habsburgs to effectively manage the Empire resulted in a power vacuum, which was filled by radical confessional alliances: the Protestant Union, founded in 1608 and led by the elector Palatine, and the Catholic League, which was founded in 1609 and led by Duke Maximilian of Bavaria.[26]

The outbreak of the war was caused by a rebellion of the Bohemian Protestant nobility against the Habsburgs as territorial rulers of the kingdom of Bohemia. From the 1560s the Habsburg hereditary lands were no longer ruled by one ruler but were split into three branches. Between 1608 and 1612 the dynasty was shaken by a severe internal crisis with the brothers and heads of these lines competing for control over each other. By this stage, about three-quarters of the inhabitants of the Habsburg hereditary lands were Protestants, but the dynasty remained Catholic. During this Brothers' Quarrel, each side was forced to make considerable concessions of religious and political rights to the Protestant nobles of their territories in return for money and support. Most famous among these was the 'Letter of Majesty' granted to the Bohemian nobles, which put them in a very influential, autonomous position and granted the subjects of Bohemia extensive rights of Protestant worship.[27]

After the successful power grab by one of the brothers, Matthias, the dynasty began to scale back the concessions granted to the nobles earlier, and to crack down on Protestantism, by denying Protestants access to public office and by equating loyalty to the dynasty with adherence to the Catholic religion. A certain parallel could be argued to exist here with the recent power grab effected by the Saudi crown prince and de facto ruler, Muhammad bin Salman, along with the overturning of traditional privileges by elite groups. Increased pressure on the rights of the Bohemian nobles led directly to the defenestration of Prague on 23 May 1618, which was carried out by the radical wing of Bohemian nobles, all of whom had been excluded from political office by the Habsburgs on account of their religion.[28]

Interpretations of the Thirty Years War

The Thirty Years War has often been portrayed as a religious war, especially until its phase of increased Europeanisation from 1635.[29] In its simplest form, this portrayal is misleading.[30] There was no uniform confessional solidarity in the war's alliances. The Protestant elector of Saxony fought on the side of the Catholic Emperor for most of the war, while Catholic France supported Protestant Sweden against the Emperor, for example. There were also cases in which Protestants carried out massacres of other Protestants. A leading historian of the war has argued that in considering the role of the religious factor in the war, it is necessary to distinguish between militants, or extremists, and moderates, because everyone was religious to a greater or lesser extent.[31] The extremists saw religious goals as within their grasp, whereas moderates were more pragmatic and viewed the realisation of religious goals as being a distant possibility. Militants were usually not in positions of power, but were instead observers and commentators such as clerics and writers. There were some notable exceptions, such as the Elector Palatine Frederick V, who had a tremendous impact on the course of events, through his religiously informed decision to accept the Bohemian crown and his subsequent refusal to compromise after he had been driven out of Prague and into exile. For the majority of political actors, this was not a holy war designed to extirpate a rival faith, or even to destroy the enemy, unlike the wars against the Turks. However, the war was undeniably related to confession, not in the sense of its being a crusade or holy war, but in the sense that it was fought over those parts of the Imperial constitution which mainly regulated the confessional balance and the modes of confessional coexistence. Coexistence per se was hardly questioned. Sectarian animosity was not the only driver, but it certainly existed, and it merged with other factors. In both the early seventeenth-century Germany and the early twenty-first-century Middle East, the quest for security has become increasingly sectarianised, as it was and is assumed that one will find automatic allies among co-religionists. This encouraged the trend of sectarianism to develop its own dynamic. However, equally as important as the religious factor in the Empire, if not more so, were the power-political and constitutional contests of regional hegemony and rival conceptions of the constitutional order. In the Holy Roman Empire, these related to the balance of power between Emperor and Imperial Estates on the one hand (centralised Imperial monarchy vs a decentralised, more federal estates-based constitution), and between Imperial Estates and their subjects within their territories on the other hand.[32] For all parties, the background of sectarian tension and hostility contributed to the overall mood of mistrust and fear, and permitted misrepresentation and miscalculation about the motives and actions of the other side, assisting powerfully in the movement towards war. These phenomena are also familiar in the contemporary Middle East.

The war is also often described as having de-coupled from rational, interests-based political direction—as having been a descent into an 'all-destructive fury', with Germans largely as the victims and Germany as the punching bag of the European great powers, especially during the last 18 years of the war.[33] But, as numerous historians have shown, the war was not out of control (or at least not wholly), as it was under political direction throughout and there were negotiations for peace running in parallel to the fighting throughout the war.[34] But it was undoubtedly terribly destructive and intense. Around a third of the German population died, mainly as an indirect result of military operations, including disease and starvation, as opposed to combat deaths (as is the case in Yemen now), and in some areas the population loss was over two-thirds.[35]

Another point of interpretation is the extent to which the war was an international war, or whether it was primarily a German war. Several historians have argued that it should not even be viewed as a discrete conflict because it was merely one theatre of a broader long-term contest between the Habsburgs and France as part of a general crisis of the seventeenth century.[36] The historiographical consensus now is that it was a distinct war with its own causes, course and consequences, and it has been shown that the terminology of a 'thirty years war' was not a retrospective construct by historians at all. Instead it was already used by contemporaries, who started counting year by year.[37] The war was mainly centred on Empire throughout, and was fought over issues of the Imperial constitution—especially, although not exclusively, those related to its confessional aspects. It started as an Imperial civil war and many of the same issues were at stake even after the foreign interventions. However, it *did* become irreversibly Europeanised or internationalised from the 1630s, in the sense that peace could not simply be made among Germans themselves within the Empire—the foreign crown would need to come to an accommodation with them too.[38]

This debate is of some interest to our purposes of proposing a Westphalian solution for the Middle East. The recognition of a unity, and of the existence of interpenetrating links between analogous past processes which in some ways seemed like several separate conflicts, can also help us to see the similar links between current crises in the Middle East and lead to the conclusion that they are part of a single story.[39]

From local rebellion to Imperial civil war: the Bohemian–Palatine phase, 1618–23

The defenestration of Prague as a symbolic act of rebellion came unexpectedly to the Habsburgs; they had recently demobilised their army and were in a precarious financial situation.[40] Following the deposition of the Habsburg king Ferdinand and the death of the Emperor Matthias in March 1619 (he was succeeded by the deposed king of Bohemia as Emperor Ferdinand II), the Bohemian territorial estates joined forces with those of other Austrian territories. The rebellion has been described as a state-building war, similar to that of the Netherlands in the 1560s.[41] A possible parallel in the current Middle East was the attempted state-building of the Islamic State by seizing territory in Syria and Iraq.[42]

At this stage the conflict remained localised within the Habsburg hereditary territories. But the decision of the Elector Palatine Frederick V to accept the Bohemian crown offered to him by the estates was an act of rebellion by a leading Imperial (as opposed to territorial) Estate, i.e. a German prince, and amounted to a de facto declaration of war by the head of the radical Protestant party in the Empire against the Emperor. The decision therefore caused the escalation of the conflict to the level of the Empire, spreading the war to the west and south of Germany. This widening of the conflict presented the Habsburgs with a problem, because defeating the Bohemian and Austrian rebels was no longer sufficient. The elector Palatine needed to be dealt with, too.[43]

The Emperor's financial problems and his lack of a standing army meant he needed external support against the rebelling estates within his own lands and against the Palatinate. His Spanish Habsburg relatives decided to intervene decisively in 1619, in order to ensure the safety of the Spanish Road, and in the hope that supporting Ferdinand II in the Empire would lead to rapid victory, and then to Austrian assistance against the Dutch in return.[44] More important, and more consequential for the further development of the war, was the support received by the Emperor from Duke Maximilian of Bavaria, along with the forces of the Catholic League which he headed, and from Saxony. The elector Palatine and new king of Bohemia, on the other hand, failed to win substantial support from either the other members of the Protestant Union (which declined to support him in 1620, and finally dissolved the following year) or from Protestant European powers. As a result, the coalition of the Emperor, Bavaria, the Catholic League, Spain and Saxony defeated the Bohemian rebels at the battle of the White Mountain in 1620, and occupied the Palatinate. The Winter King, Frederick V, as he then became known, was chased into exile in the Netherlands. By 1623 the Emperor's enemies were defeated, but this was a borrowed victory, because he had relied heavily on Spanish, Saxon and, more importantly, Bavarian support.[45]

The significance of this borrowed victory was that Saxon and Bavarian support came at a high price. In return for Saxon assistance, the Emperor was forced to cede territory in Lusatia to the Saxon elector. More consequential for the subsequent course of the war was the price that Bavaria had exacted. Duke Maximilian was promised the transfer of the Palatine electoral dignity to Bavaria, along with the occupied territory of the Upper Palatinate. Following a fast-tracked judicial procedure at the Imperial Aulic Council, the elector Palatine was declared to be under Imperial ban, and was to be dispossessed, with the usual litigation procedures deemed superfluous on account of the 'notoriety' of his rebellion against the Emperor. This cleared the way for the transfer of his electoral dignity and title to the duke of Bavaria, which occurred in 1623 without the consent of the other electors and against the advice of the Emperor's allies, Saxony and Spain.[46]

Such unilateral redistribution of lands and dignities itself perpetuated the war because it caused new grievances, including fears of an overweening Imperial authority and suspicions of Imperial centralisation with the attendant threat to German liberties. These grievances were then used by the exiled elector Palatine and the exiled Bohemian and Austrian rebels in order to rally opposition forces and attract funding from England and the Dutch in order to pay for armies of mercenaries under princes who at times acted as military contractors, such as Ernst von Mansfeld, Christian von Braunschweig and the margrave of Baden. These armies kept the war against the Emperor going. Despite the judicial veneer furnished by the Emperor's supreme court, the dispossession of 'notorious rebels', such as the elector Palatine and other Protestant princes who supported him, for the benefit of princes who had assisted the Emperor was legally highly problematic and probably unconstitutional, causing resentment which prolonged the war. But the Emperor had little choice because of his military weakness and his previous reliance upon Bavarian support.[47]

From Imperial victory to Imperial triumph: the Lower Saxon and Danish phase, 1623–9

Despite heavy reliance on extensive support from Bavaria, Spain, Saxony and others, the Emperor's position seemed strong by 1623 and, with this victory, the war came to a temporary halt—until the Danish intervention. The king of Denmark was also an Imperial prince as duke of Holstein, and a member of the Lower Saxon circle (district). King Christian IV, along with many of the princes of the circle, viewed the strengthening of the Emperor and the presence of large Imperial and Catholic League armies to the immediate south of the circle frontier as a threat. This, together with the distraction of Denmark's great rival, Sweden, due to a new war against Poland, emboldened Christian IV to intervene against the Emperor, on the side of the exiled elector Palatine, reigniting the war in 1625.[48]

The new threat to the Emperor and his allies from the north led to the appointment of Albrecht von Wallenstein as Imperial general, who proposed a radical and novel method of war financing. He acted as a military subcontractor, creating an extraordinarily large army, which was financed by himself on credit, but served in the name of the Emperor. The army would then forcibly exact money payments from the Imperial Estates and communities in which it operated in order to pay for its upkeep. Together with the Catholic League's army under commander Johann Tserclaes Tilly, Wallenstein scored major victories against the Danes and drove them completely out of Germany. By 1629 Denmark had accepted defeat and promised not to intervene again, in return for relatively generous terms at the Peace of Lübeck. The Emperor was at the height of his power, which now extended across Germany, including into the far north.[49]

In the hubris of victory, the Emperor overreached himself with the Edict of Restitution in 1629. This measure sought to impose a narrow Catholic interpretation of the Peace of Augsburg by ordering the restitution of all Catholic Church goods and property that had been confiscated since 1552, contrary to the Augsburg peace. The measure is often portrayed as having been driven by religious bigotry and as the result of an extreme Catholic position. Recent research has shown that it was not the policy that the more anti-Protestant group of advisers in Vienna had wished, and it certainly was not aimed at extirpating Protestantism.[50] Nevertheless it was a major blow to the Protestants' position in the Empire—many secularisations had taken place since 1552 in spite of the terms of the Augsburg peace—and it was very unpopular among the Imperial Estates of both confessions. This was because, like the transfer of the Palatine electoral dignity and territory, it was carried out unilaterally and by Imperial decree. Most princes viewed this as a worrying sign that the Emperor was taking advantage of his unprecedented power and military ascendancy to ride roughshod over their traditional liberties—their rights to share in the government and management of the Empire, referred to at the time as the 'German liberties'. The edict alienated those important

Protestant princes who had hitherto remained loyal to the Emperor, especially the electors of Saxony and Brandenburg. This was compounded by the banning and subsequent deposition of the Protestant dukes of Mecklenburg in 1628, for allying with Denmark, and the transfer of their territories to the Catholic Wallenstein as the new duke of Mecklenburg. As had been the case with the transfer of the electoral dignity to Bavaria, this was highly questionable legally and, even among the Catholics, greatly compounded princely fears of a possible emergence of a centralised Imperial monarchy and the erosion of princely liberties. The Catholic League was also highly suspicious of Wallenstein and his alarming accretion of power.

The basic problem of the paradox of Imperial strength facing the Emperor at the end of the 1620s was the same as it had been at the beginning of the decade. Despite appearing powerful, the Emperor's lack of a large standing army compelled him to rely instead on a private military contractor (Wallenstein) who had to be rewarded and paid off, just like his princely allies in 1623. He was therefore forced to redistribute lands to his supporters in a way that was seen as a threat to the existing constitutional order, creating new grievances and a casus belli, which prolonged the war. The reaction at the electors' meeting in Regensburg in 1630 was decisive: they forced the Emperor to dismiss Wallenstein and refused to have his son elected as successor.

The Swedish intervention and the Peace of Prague, 1630–5

A new and more serious level of European escalation began with the Swedish invasion of Pomerania in 1630. While the public justification of King Gustavus Adolphus's intervention emphasised the legality of the intervention as a defensive act, along with the desire to uphold the legal rights of the princes, his true ambitions are less clear. The key factor behind the decision was likely geo-strategic in nature. Sweden considered the Emperor's expanded sphere of direct control towards the Baltic as a threat to its own ambitions for Baltic hegemony. Wallenstein's installation as duke of Mecklenburg and the seeming naval ambitions of the Emperor (Wallenstein was also proclaimed 'general of the oceanic and Baltic seas') were particularly ominous from Stockholm's perspective. This was certainly a 'red line' for the Swedes, in some ways similar to the red line that the Saudis believed was crossed with the perceived expansion of Iranian influence in Yemen through their support to the Houthi rebels. Related to this was the apparent shift in the constitutional balance towards the Emperor at the expense of the Imperial Estates. This was itself a geopolitical threat, because it was not in Sweden's interest to have as its neighbour a more centralised Holy Roman Empire which was under greater Habsburg control and more capable of external power projection. Gustavus Adolphus also portrayed himself as a saviour of Protestant and princely liberties, although the majority of Protestant princes did not wish to be saved.[51]

Sweden's intervention was supported by French subsidies upon which it depended. It was therefore also a proxy war by France against the Emperor. Sweden's military campaign was astonishingly successful, to the point of even worrying the French. They did not wish to see the Emperor's hegemony in Germany replaced by that of Protestant Sweden. Within less than two years, Gustavus Adolphus had conquered most of Germany, as far south as Bavaria. Gradually most major Protestant princes allied with Sweden or were forced to do so by the Swedish army. The Emperor's dominance vanished in just a couple of years. In the 1630s, the most intense and destructive phase of the war began, as internal rebellions within Germany were replaced by European great powers clashing directly in full-scale combat, on German soil and elsewhere.[52]

The big Swedish victory at the battle of Breitenfeld in 1631 persuaded many princes that Sweden was a viable ally, and the burning of the Protestant town of Magdeburg by the Imperial forces under Tilly in the same year also drove many Protestant princes into the arms of the Swedes. Saxony had been neutral, but now started rearming itself energetically, largely in response to the massacre at Magdeburg. It was then invaded by Imperial forces in 1631, which pushed it onto the Swedish anti-Imperial side. This facilitated the creation of a broad-based Protestant alliance under Swedish leadership in Heilbronn in 1633. By 1634, the Emperor, with support from Bavaria and Spain, had recovered and achieved a victory at Nördlingen against the Swedes and their Protestant German allies.[53]

The Emperor was now in a position of strength again, but this time he had learned the lessons from his previous mistakes in 1623 and 1628–9, and aimed at reaching a real compromise accommodation with Saxony, the leading Protestant power in the Empire, without imposing diktats or unilaterally redistributing territory. The resulting Peace of Prague of 1635 was a bilateral treaty, but its aims included the other princes, and indeed most Imperial Estates joined the arrangement, isolating Sweden. The settlement incorporated many concessions and innovations, showing the desire of the Imperialists and Saxons to achieve a lasting peace.[54] Concessions to the Protestants included the suspension of the hated Edict of Restitution, and its replacement by a completely novel peace instrument, the 'normative year'. This fixed the distribution of confessional property possession to what it had been on 12 November 1627, a date which was a compromise between the ideal dates sought by each party: it reversed the effects of both the Edict of Restitution and the victory march of Gustavus Adolphus.[55] The Peace also extended an amnesty to most princes, but not several of the original rebel princes such as the elector Palatine or the landgrave of Hessen-Kassel. The Calvinists were still not granted recognition. Significantly, the customary right of princes to enter into alliances with each other was abrogated, leading to the dissolution of the Catholic League. The aim was to make peace internally within the Empire, and then force the external crowns to retreat from Germany with the aid of a new Imperial army. The trend was clearly towards a more centralised Imperial monarchy, but the princes' desire for peace after almost twenty years of war outweighed their constitutional qualms. Sweden and France, however, were not going to be as acquiescent, although the Emperor probably missed an opportunity in 1635 to make peace with Sweden on a bilateral basis had he been willing to offer relatively moderate concessions. Instead, he banked on German unity in order to either present the crowns with a fait accompli in the hope that they would withdraw or, if necessary, confront the crowns from a position of strength.[56]

The French–Swedish phase, 1635–48

When the Peace of Prague was concluded, France had already declared war against Spain. It had fought its great rivals, the Spanish and Austrian Habsburgs, mainly by proxy throughout the 1620s and early 1630s, but in 1635 intervened directly, thus further escalating the war. The decision was ostensibly taken in response to the Spanish arrest of the elector of Trier, a French protégé, and the resulting official declaration of war was only directed against Spain.[57] The French alliance with the Dutch—directed against the Spanish Netherlands—and with Savoy, Mantua and Parma—directed against Spanish Milan—completed Cardinal Richelieu's anti-Habsburg drive.[58] The French declaration of war against Spain was not immediately followed by war against the Emperor. It was only in 1636 that King Louis XIII and Ferdinand II broke off diplomatic relations. Although the French did increasingly send their own armies into Germany to fight an undeclared war against the Emperor, the onus was still on proxy war: continued subsidies to Sweden and the purchase of the service of the ducal military contractor Bernard of Weimar.[59]

An important emphasis of Richelieu's foreign policy during this period was to bind Sweden ever closer to France in order to ensure that it would not need to shoulder alone the burden of the effort against the Emperor, and the Habsburgs in general. Richelieu clearly recognised the danger that Protestant setbacks posed for France's anti-Habsburg strategy and the position of France in Europe. In late 1634 he warned that 'it is certain that if the Protestant party [i.e. Sweden and its princely allies] is entirely ruined, the brunt of the power of the House of Austria will fall on France'.[60] At some stages, such as the period after the crushing Swedish defeat at Nördlingen, and again in 1640, there was a real risk that Sweden could exit the war, if it had been offered adequate financial compensation and achieved some guarantees of princely and Protestant rights in the Empire. But because Sweden and France were not included in the negotiations leading to the Peace of Prague, there was little chance that they would consider it an honourable peace. This exclusion of some of the main stakeholders and warring parties from the negotiations and resulting peace treaty is the reason for the failure of the Prague peace settlement to end the war.

In the years following the election of the new, more pragmatic emperor, Ferdinand III, in 1637, French involvement in the war in Germany increased. By concluding a firm alliance with Sweden at Hamburg in 1638 (reaffirmed in 1641), in which the allies agreed not to make a separate peace, Richelieu had achieved his main goal of safeguarding France from isolation against the Habsburgs. It was in fact the strength of this alliance, and the Franco-Swedish insistence on including their respective princely allies in peace talks, that necessitated a multilateral peace congress, and that prevented the implementation of the Emperor's preferred peace plan of a set of bilateral talks and treaties. In 1639–40, Spain experienced a series of disasters, including the loss of Catalonia and Portugal following French-sponsored rebellions there, and a major financial crisis. This occurred on top of the fact that Madrid was already embroiled in an increasingly costly two-front war against France and the Netherlands, which encouraged Spain to join the peace negotiations. Spain's domestic and international troubles allowed France increasingly to shift its military efforts to the Empire.[61]

During its last ten years, the war reached something of a stalemate, although on the whole the position of the Franco-Swedish allies became stronger while the Emperor's position worsened. During this time, much of the fighting in the Empire was aimed at imposing each side's own conception of what an eventual peace should look like, and how it was to be achieved. The Emperor sought to inflict defeats on Sweden or France in order to force either into a separate peace, so as to be able to face the other from a position of strength and improve his chances during the subsequent bilateral negotiations. The crowns wished to force the Emperor to attend a multilateral congress at which their princely allies would be represented, while also aiming at reaching preliminary accommodations with individual princes so that these would no longer support the Emperor's war effort. The Emperor was forced to make concessions as a result of major defeats, mainly inflicted by the Swedes, at the second battle of Breitenfeld in 1642 and Jankau in 1645, and as a result of a renewed assault in 1644—coordinated with Sweden—on Austrian-ruled Hungary by the prince of Transylvania, Georg Rákóczi, an Ottoman vassal.[62]

4

THE PEACE CONGRESS OF MÜNSTER AND OSNABRÜCK (1643–1648) AND THE WESTPHALIAN ORDER (1648–1806)

Pax optima rerum—Peace is the highest boon

Inscription on a medal minted to commemorate the conclusion of the Peace of Westphalia, Münster, 1648

In order to resolve regional conflicts such as the one between the GCC states and Iran, the different parties can look at Europe for examples on how to resolve historic rivalries and how peace agreements such as the Peace of Westphalia were concluded.

Hossein Mousavian, research scholar, Woodrow Wilson School of Public and International Affairs, Princeton University; workshop participant of 'A Westphalia for the Middle East', 2016–17[1]

Why did it take so long for the Congress to open?

Before addressing the negotiations at the peace congress, it is appropriate to ask why it took so long to reach the point at which a functioning peace congress was convened, because the form that the congress eventually assumed was related to the longevity of the war and the failure of previous peace efforts.

According to one historian, the longevity of the war can be explained by three main factors: a repeated failure of crisis containment, a conflation of methods to achieve war goals with a necessity to sustain the war itself, and the necessity of granting concessions from a position of strength. As explained in the last chapter, the Habsburgs were almost bankrupt at the beginning of the war and it came unexpectedly upon them. With no large standing army, they required support from third parties, mainly Bavaria and Saxony, but the Emperor was required to pay for this assistance with enfeoffments and dignities. For this purpose, the Emperor could exploit his position as highest judge and feudal overlord by branding opponents—from whom lands and dignities were taken for redistribution—as rebels and imposing criminal penalties on them. A similar blanket labelling of 'terrorists' in order to discredit opposition has been used by various actors in the Middle East and beyond. This action of the Emperor in turn created new grievances which sustained the war and contributed to escalation through intervention because outside powers were concerned at the shifting constitutional balance in the Empire. A similar method was adopted within Habsburg hereditary lands. The confiscation of rebel lands and their redistribution to loyal nobles created the problem of exiles, with nothing left to lose and everything to gain, who helped rally anti-Habsburg forces and organise mercenary armies and interventions. They also represented a cause, around which opponents could rally and legitimise intervention.[2]

Because all sides had stopped paying their armies and officers through regular channels by the 1620s, they relied instead on distributing captured land and living off the land. This was an obstacle to peace because such lands would need to be returned yet the armies would have to be compensated financially if they were to give up these spoils of war which they had been given instead of regular salaries. This was especially vital in the case of Sweden, whose armies depended completely on such payments, and this became a major factor in delaying conclusion of peace. Also, the fact that it was fought with the classical precepts of a just war in mind meant that the war was aimed at rectifying specific perceived injustices to produce a negotiated settlement, as opposed to the total destruction of the enemy in order to procure an unconditional surrender, as was the case in the Second World War, for example. This made it harder to win the war quickly as concessions would need to be negotiated and backed up by positions of military advantage, though not necessarily total military supremacy.[3]

Part of the reason for the seeming interminability of the war was that it took a long time for the major actors to reach, by trial and error, the required methods and practices of peacemaking. An important discovery of recent research is that negotiations for peace did not only begin at Münster and Osnabrück. Peace negotiations were conducted among various actors, on a bilateral or multilateral basis, or through the meditation of third parties, almost throughout the entire duration of the war.[4] There were also several actual peace treaties and conferences before the opening of the Westphalian congress, which of course failed to achieve a lasting peace. This was a reflection of the peace-oriented culture of that age, which might sound startling, given that there was almost perennial warfare in the seventeenth century.[5] However, throughout the period, and throughout the Thirty Years War, the most important actors viewed peace as the chief norm regulating inter-state relations among Christian states and the basis of the international order, not least because it was seen as divinely ordained. War was not seen as an end in itself, nor was it glorified. It was justified as a means towards achieving peace. In almost all propaganda and public statements, the desire for peace and the willingness to enter into peace negotiations were emphasised.[6] This basic normative consensus was an important precondition for the many initiatives of peace diplomacy and for the final convening of the Westphalian congress. It is also reflected in the willingness of the actors to engage in innovative diplomatic practices and to disregard certain precepts of international law in the pursuit of peace. An example is the talks conducted between the Emperor and the Bohemian rebels, mediated by the elector of Saxony in 1618 and 1619. Legally, the rebels were the Emperor's subjects and therefore diplomatic negotiations between them could not take place, but both parties engaged in them nevertheless, not only in the hope of achieving a resolution to the crisis, but also in order to be seen by the (princely and aristocratic) public as undertaking necessary steps in pursuit of peace.[7]

How, then, can one explain why this underlying normative emphasis on the value of peace failed to achieve an actual peace settlement for so long? It has been emphasised that after the European escalation, peace would need to include an accommodation with the intervening European powers as well. As argued in the preceding chapter, the Peace of Prague largely failed because the Empire did not exist in a geopolitical vacuum, and the external powers were not included in the peace process. Similarly, the peace conference of Cologne failed because it failed to include the Protestant powers and princes. It had been convened in 1636 and 1637 by the Pope as a peace initiative between the major Catholic powers. But because this attempted to address only one component part of the overall conflict, while leaving major conflict areas unsettled, it was bound to fail to achieve an overall peace. The importance of including the Protestant powers was made clear at this time when Sweden displayed its renewed dynamism and scored a big victory against the Imperials at the battle of Wittstock in 1636.

A fundamental reason for the continuous failure to achieve peace was that there were different conceptions of what kind of peace there should be. As mentioned earlier, the Imperialists wanted a separate German settlement between princes and Emperor, and to then deal with foreign crowns in turn. This was attempted, but failed after the Peace of Prague. The Spaniards were also fundamentally sceptical about the prospects of a multilateral congress, which they expected to be incapable of solving all the complicated interconnected conflicts at a single stroke. They claimed that a congress would actually inhibit the achievement of peace and argued that congress diplomacy amounted to an 'eternalisation of war'.[8] Richelieu's concept of a universal peace settlement which would solve all interrelated and concurrent conflicts in Europe simultaneously was fundamentally different and was also a novel idea in early modern diplomacy, which required the innovative peace instrument of the multilateral congress. Following Richelieu's death at the end of 1642, this basic policy direction was continued by the new French premier, Cardinal Jules Mazarin. Faced with an unshakably tight Franco-Swedish alliance, the Emperor was forced to accede to the French model by agreeing to the multilateral peace congress at the Hamburg peace preliminaries in 1641. Over the course of 1643–5, when more and more delegations of European powers and German princes began arriving in Münster and Osnabrück, it started to become clear that the French goal of a universal congress was being realised.

Despite the considerable achievements of the congress, the hoped-for universal peace remained elusive, because it failed to resolve Spanish–French differences. When this became clear, the congress risked dissolving and reached a point of crisis, which was compounded by the departure of the chief Imperial plenipotentiary, but was saved by the efforts of a group of envoys of middling princes, the 'Third Party'. This grouping managed to force their larger partners back to the negotiating table and conclude the final peace. The result was neither a particular German peace, nor a universal peace, but an intermediate solution of an internationally guaranteed security zone for central Europe, in which the Holy Roman Empire was removed from ongoing war in the West and its internal arrangements were guaranteed mutually by all powers including the foreign crowns.[9]

Characteristics of the Congress

The congress was highly innovative. It was the first ever multilateral peace congress, with 109 embassies representing the Emperor, numerous kings, republics and princes, as well as 140 Imperial Estates. The cost of the congress has been estimated at 3.2 million Reichstaler.[10] As a diplomatic meeting of such dimensions was unprecedented, there was little guidance as to how to conduct the negotiations and other proceedings. The convening of a single conference at two different locations had been arranged in the Hamburg peace preliminaries and was also novel. The main reason for this was to avoid the Papal delegation having to encounter Protestant delegations, and to avoid ceremonial precedence disputes between France and Sweden. Therefore, the Emperor and Sweden negotiated at Osnabrück, whereas the Habsburg powers (Emperor and Spain) negotiated with France at Münster. The Dutch and the Spaniards also negotiated at Münster. Princes of both confessions were represented at both congress towns. The locations were therefore not neatly divided by religion, although more Catholic powers and princes were negotiating in the Catholic town of Münster and more Protestants in the largely Protestant town of Osnabrück.[11]

Mediators were planned for both towns: Venice and the Papacy in Münster, Denmark in Osnabrück.[12] Sweden attacked its long-standing rival, Denmark, in 1643, in order to eliminate it as a potentially hostile mediator, among other reasons. This war had its desired effect, because according to prevailing concepts of the law of nature and nations, a mediator had to be neutral. Yet over the course of the negotiations, the parties at Münster resorted to the innovative step of using a non-neutral mediator. The Dutch—allied to France—were added as additional mediators in Franco-Spanish negotiations, despite being at war with Spain, because the negotiations under the mediation of Papal envoy Fabio Chigi were not making sufficient progress.[13] It was recognised that the Dutch had a greater vested self-interest in peace, and could furthermore put more effective pressure on the French as their allies than the neutral but distant Pope.

The involved parties had set the bar for success very high. The congress was aimed at solving all interrelated conflicts at once, and the obstacles that needed to be overcome were very high. Some of the participating powers had never even recognised each other's status, such as the Papal mediator, who viewed the Protestants as heretics, and the French, who did not recognise the election of Ferdinand III as Emperor, because their close ally and protégé, the archbishop-elector of Trier, Philipp Christoph von Sötern, had not taken part in the election as he had been imprisoned by the Spanish in 1635. The Emperor reluctantly had to accept participation of the Imperial Estates—his own immediate subjects and vassals—as negotiating parties in an international peace congress, which he perceived as a slight to the dignity of his office.

This points to a fundamental disagreement among the major powers during the early stages of the congress, namely the question of the scope of participation. According to the Emperor, the internal problems relating to the confessional and constitutional disputes within the Holy Roman Empire had already been definitively settled at the Peace of Prague. He agreed to the congress at Westphalia because of the refusal of France and Sweden to make peace separately. But he certainly did not wish to see the Imperial Estates represented at the congress, except for the electors, whose dispatch of envoys to an international congress had been approved at the electors' congress of Regensburg in 1636. According to the Emperor's conception of the Imperial constitution, the head of the Empire, as the monarch, was entitled to represent the Empire as a whole, and domestic affairs relating to the Empire's constitution and confessional arrangements were to be negotiated between the Emperor and the princes at the Imperial Diet, or the electors' congress, not at an international peace congress. But the foreign crowns, Sweden in particular, increasingly pressed for the inclusion not only of their allies among the princes (which the Emperor might have been able to suffer), but of all Imperial Estates. They were energetically encouraged and pressed to do so by the belligerent landgravine of Hessen-Kassel, Amalia Elisabeth, who was supported on this point by Frederick William, the 'Great Elector' of Brandenburg. The Swedish negotiator Johann Adler Salvius noted that the exclusion of the Estates from the negotiations would amount to 'a path towards [the Emperor's] absolute domination and the servitude of the Estates. The crowns will prevent this. Their security consists of the liberty of the German Estates.'[14] The envoys of many of the Imperial Estates began trickling in to the congress towns at the instigation of the foreign powers and in defiance of the Emperor's instructions for them not to attend. Ultimately it was the Emperor's crushing defeat at the battle of Jankau in 1645 that forced him to agree to the crowns' and many of the princes' demand, and to send an official invitation to all the Imperial Estates to attend the congress.[15] The inclusion of the Imperial Estates was the first major political result of the congress.[16] It thereby became simultaneously a site of negotiations for an international peace treaty and also a constitutional convention for the Holy Roman Empire, which was another innovation in international state practice and in the law of nations.

The extensive conflicts over diplomatic precedence and protocol were another peculiar characteristic of the congress of Westphalia.[17] Disputes over which envoys would walk out farthest towards an arriving embassy in order to greet the other envoy, for example, could lead to major disputes and at times risk derailing the congress. Such issues of ritual symbolism relating to rank and ceremonial might appear ridiculous to posterity, but the latest research has shown their importance—they were not an expression of individual personal vanity and pettiness on the part of the envoys, but rather a reflection and manifestation of the political conflicts over which the war itself was being fought, such as the relative rank and status, or the sovereignty, or lack thereof, of a particular power. The role of ceremonial was especially important because in early modern Europe sovereignty was not just a quality inherent in a particular polity, but was also attached to an individual ruler as a form of social status.[18] Interestingly, ceremonial rank disputes receded over the course of the congress. The diplomats became increasingly pragmatic and started to recognise that a rigid insistence on one's own interpretation of ceremonial could hinder progress in the negotiations. This points to the crucial factor of the negotiators' willingness to be innovative and to compromise.[19]

Why did it take so long for the Congress to conclude a peace?

The Westphalian congress was recently described as 'the longest continuous peace conference in modern history'.[20] The congress had no official opening date, but embassies of several powers began arriving from 1643. The arrival of the head of the Emperor's embassy, the chief plenipotentiary Count Maximilian von Trauttmansdorff,[21] in November 1645 marked the beginning of the main phase of the congress, when negotiations were conducted in earnest. The peace treaties were only signed on 24 October 1648 and ratifications exchanged the following year (18 February). A simple reason for the long duration of the negotiations is that it was a negotiated peace, not an imposed peace as the result of a surrender, as after the First and Second World Wars.

One historian has argued that the final conclusion of the peace treaty remained elusive for so long because of conflicting conceptions of the minimum conditions which were necessary for the ending of the war and the creation of honourable peace conditions, the idea of the so-called *pax honesta* (i.e. honest or honourable peace). This early modern princely and aristocratic conception of honour was highly important and often led to a willingness to continue fighting in the hope of achieving one more victory, which would then improve one's position at the negotiating table and increase the chances of obtaining more honourable stipulations.[22] This points to another important reason, namely that the fighting continued in parallel to the negotiations throughout the congress. Changing military fortunes on the battlefield had a considerable impact on negotiations and vice versa.[23] Other reasons include the internal political struggles among the negotiating parties, especially in France, Sweden and the Netherlands. This led to divisions and conflicting messages from individual members of the same embassies, resulting in confusion and delay caused by the need to achieve clarity over the actual position of interlocutors.

Additionally, the fact that all Imperial Estates were entitled to attend the negotiations (and many did) had the effect of multiplying the number of negotiating parties by at least a factor of twenty. Its consequent dimensions as a 'mammoth congress'[24] arguably complicated proceedings and delayed the process of achieving a consensus or compromise. On the other hand, it was precisely the inclusivity of the congress which was a key reason for its eventual success, and in the final stages of the congress the consensus-oriented Imperial Estates of the 'Third Party', who displayed a greater willingness to compromise than the European great powers, played a crucial role in driving the peace process to a conclusion.

Modes of negotiations and Congress life

Contrary to what the term 'congress' suggests, there were never any plenary meetings in which all delegates met in one big room. The format of the negotiations was complicated, and this was not only on account of ceremonial disputes. In Münster, the Spanish and French negotiators never officially met face to face, but only negotiated indirectly and largely in writing through the Venetian and Papal mediators, as stipulated in the Hamburg peace preliminaries. This also prolonged negotiations, not least because of the requisite translation work. In addition, as mentioned above, the Dutch were active as mediators between Spain and France between autumn 1646 and spring 1647, and from the end of 1647 until the summer of 1648.[25] Negotiations in Osnabrück were less rigid because the Swedes, having knocked out the Danes as the designated mediators, preferred direct negotiations with the envoys of the Emperor and of the Imperial Estates. Münster became the location at which most of the international terms were negotiated, whereas talks in Osnabrück focused more on German religious and constitutional affairs, largely because Sweden had a greater interest in them than France, and because of the more numerous presence of princely envoys there.[26]

The presence of the Imperial Estates complicated the course of the negotiations because they arranged themselves along the complex lines to which they were accustomed at the Imperial Diet. This meant that they were divided between three 'colleges' of electors, princes and cities. But because the Imperial Estates were represented at both Münster and Osnabrück, this tripartite division was replicated twice. On top of this, they also informally grouped themselves by religion, into the Protestant Corpus Evangelicorum and the Catholic Corpus Catholicorum. Over the course of the congress, these confessional blocs became the main organising principle and negotiating unit for the Imperial Estates. They gradually broke loose from the rigid procedural rules that they had started with, and instead adopted more practical modes of negotiation, which came to fruition with the success of the Third Party.

A further complicating factor during the negotiations was that the war had not been a simple struggle between two coalitions. The lines of conflict, enmity and alliance were much less straightforward. Sweden was at war with the Emperor, but not with his Spanish allies. Sweden and the Dutch Republic were both allied with France, but not with each other. The Franco-Dutch alliance was only directed against Spain, and the Dutch were not at war with the Emperor. Such complex conflict constellations again have similarities with the current situation in the Middle East. There are considerable divisions within the Sunni camp—between Qatar and Saudi Arabia, for example; and other Sunnis in the Gulf region also resent Saudi hegemony. In Syria and elsewhere, the Turks are at war with the Kurdish People's Protection Units and other Kurdish groups, who are allied to Turkey's own ally, the United States. Another major belligerent in Syria, Russia, is on relatively good terms with both of the major regional rivals, Iran and Saudi Arabia, despite fighting the latter's proxies and allies in Syria.[27]

An important feature of the seventeenth-century negotiations was that each party set out clearly its own interests, or demands, at the beginning. This was reflected in the initial drafts and aims that were exchanged by the negotiating parties, the so-called 'propositions' of peace. However, there was no transparency from the outset in terms of revealing the maximum concessions that any party was willing to tolerate. These were communicated from the court of the chief negotiator in great secrecy. Given that it was a negotiated settlement, the process which was generally adopted was that each party would present a maximum level of demands and a minimum level of concessions at the outset, before a drawn-out haggling procedure eventually produced the agreed terms.[28] The envoys at the congress were not simply executive organs of their home governments, but were often leading politicians and high-ranking nobles in their own right, who possessed considerable decision-making freedom. The Emperor's chief negotiator, Trauttmansdorff, for example, was the head of the Imperial government. The prevailing difficulty of communications in seventeenth-century Europe made a degree of delegation of decision-making unavoidable, and arguably helped towards peace.

The latest research into the congress of Westphalia has underlined the importance of informal modes of communication between the envoys, including non-verbal ones. Social gatherings and events such as theatre and music performances, often centred around leading plenipotentiaries' wives, to some extent fostered a sense of cohesion among the envoys. As they were resident in close proximity to each other for many years, in often less comfortable circumstances than they were accustomed to, the envoys eventually formed their own separate sense of community. They often experienced shared hardships such as illness. This, together with their more-or-less independent decision-making capacity, turned them into an effective 'peace party' in their own right, which often had the effect of pushing their home courts into a more conciliatory or compromising stance than they would have adopted otherwise.[29] The congress therefore developed its own dynamic.[30]

Topics of negotiations and the role of the Third Party

The main topics of negotiations, which were deemed by the participants to be essential in order to reach a peace settlement, were grouped together under several headings. These concerned both 'international' terms, which regulated the relationship between the great powers and the redistribution of territory between them, and 'internal' matters relating to the religious and constitutional arrangements of the Holy Roman Empire, as well as a mixture of the two. That the domestic constitutional laws of a state were subject to international renegotiation was highly unusual and probably unprecedented. The various topics were largely treated in parallel. The negotiation headings included 'satisfaction and compensation', which referred to the cession of territory by the Empire to France and Sweden, ostensibly as 'compensation' for their military efforts and services in defence of German princely liberties. It also included the cash payment that Sweden was demanding to cover the costs of clearing officers' and soldiers' back pay and decommissioning its numerous troops stationed in the Empire. This was effectively a payment of reparations. Negotiations over these terms took up a high proportion of the overall deliberations.[31]

'Amnesty and restitution' referred to the restoration of rights and territories to the status quo ante bellum and was seen as an integral part of restoring peace. Amnesty was the pledge not to assign blame for the ills of the war, and to consign all wrong-doing to 'perpetual oblivion'. It therefore promised mutual immunity from blame and from post-war prosecution for war crimes committed. The central component of restitution was the return of territories and dignities that numerous parties had been deprived of as a result of occupation, but also as a consequence of Imperial judicial proceedings, such as having been placed under the 'ban'. Of course, this was only selectively applied, and much of the negotiation on these points related to the numerous exemptions and special arrangements. The end result was far from a return to the status quo ante bellum of 1618, with the Bavarian elector being able to retain his substantial gains of 1621–3 at the expense of the Palatinate, for example, and the rebels within the Habsburg hereditary lands being excluded from restitution and amnesty entirely.[32]

Among the internal constitutional topics, the rights of the Imperial Estates—which featured so prominently in the later denigration of the Peace and were in some ways the progenitor of the Westphalian myth—were wrapped up quite promptly at the congress and without much controversy, as they merely reaffirmed existing rights.[33] French attempts to alter the constitutional balance in favour of the princes, by prohibiting the election of an Emperor designate ('king of the Romans') during the lifetime of a reigning Emperor, were rejected by the Imperial Estates, which were therefore less hostile towards their Emperor than the foreign crowns had wished. Much more contested and bitter were the negotiations surrounding the main aspect of the Imperial constitutional terms, namely the confessional laws and arrangements.

The negotiations on the topic of the religious terms were drawn out over almost three years.[34] A Swedish proposition of June 1645 demanded that the religious terms of the Imperial constitution be renegotiated. After the Emperor accepted this in principle, the Catholic and Protestant Imperial Estates negotiated directly with each other from late 1645 to mid-1646 without making progress. After asking Trauttmansdorff for mediation, he soon took over the negotiations with the Protestants himself, while periodically touching base with the Catholics. Over the course of these negotiations, the Protestant Imperial Estates shifted their position from an emphasis on the abolition of the Ecclesiastical Reservation and an insistence on the Right of Reformation for all rulers, towards an emphasis on the confessional rights of the subject populations within the territories and therefore a limitation of the Right of Reformation.[35] This could best be achieved through the 'normative year' the eventual adoption of which, after much numerical haggling, can be rated as a success of the diplomacy of electoral Saxony and other moderate, Imperially loyal Lutheran Estates.[36] As Catholic hostility towards the Emperor's concessions grew, Trauttmansdorff began direct negotiations with the Swedes, who in turn consulted the Protestant Imperial Estates. He presented a draft as the result of his negotiations, the so-called Trauttmansdorffianum, in June 1647. At this stage the Imperial Estates were paralysed by bitter infighting between Catholics and Protestants, between Lutherans and Calvinists, and between those Catholics willing and those unwilling to compromise. The Corpus Catholicorum rejected Trauttmansdorff's draft and he left the congress in July 1647.[37]

The congress had reached a crisis point, compounded by the growing realisation that Spain and France would not be able to reach a peace. At this crucial moment, in late 1647 and early 1648 the cross-confessional grouping of the Third Party, consisting of Imperial Estates willing to compromise and guided by the recognition of the urgent necessity of peace (Saxony, Brandenburg, Mainz, Trier, Würzburg, Bamberg and Braunschweig-Lüneburg, among others), took over the initiative. Such a cross-confessional grouping was a complete innovation and its members proposed a new mode of negotiating: the Swedish and Imperial envoys, assisted by the consensus-oriented Imperial Estates of both confessions, should negotiate the outstanding religious disagreements individually, and sign an agreement on each in turn before moving on to the next. Such agreements should be binding for all. This pragmatic and innovative method was adopted and had the desired effect of shutting out the intransigent and uncompromising hardliners. It was crucial in reaching a final agreement on religious matters in March–April 1648, in direct negotiations between the Swedes and the Emperor. The final draft of the religious terms bears a very close resemblance to the Trauttmansdorffianum.[38] The Third Party was also instrumental in overcoming the last major hurdle of the peace: the French demand that the Emperor be prohibited from assisting Spain in its ongoing war against France. This was a clause on which France was insisting if it was to sign a treaty with the Emperor but not Spain, and the Imperial Estates knew that peace in the Empire depended on the Emperor's agreement to this clause. The Emperor had long refused to countenance such a limitation to freedom of action in foreign policy. But by late summer 1648 the Third Party was able to fully exploit the Emperor's dire military position (Prague was in the process of being occupied by the Swedes), and to make it clear to him that he would be totally isolated in the Empire if he refused to sign off on the 'non-assistance clause'. Following an important report by his ministers in early October 1648, in which they recommended an acceptance of the draft treaty devised by the Imperial Estates and France, and therefore a break with Spain, the Emperor finally relented and agreed to the non-assistance clause.[39] Ferdinand III knew that his emperorship would be at risk if he completely isolated himself from the Imperial Estates. The non-assistance clause enjoyed a much greater consensus among the princes than the confessional terms, because they believed that the Emperor was delaying the conclusion of peace simply for the sake of his Spanish relatives.[40]

The tortuous and meandering negotiations leading to the final religious and constitutional terms, as well as those stipulating satisfaction, amnesty and restitution, have been painstakingly reconstructed elsewhere.[41] But before summarising the eventual treaty terms, it is worth exploring in more detail the establishment of the guarantee clauses. Not only has this topic of negotiation been neglected in most of the existing historical works, it is also one of the most relevant from the perspective of a proposed Westphalian peace for the Middle East.

The question of how to secure and safeguard the peace through a guarantee (*assecuratio pacis*) played an important role during the negotiations.[42] Even before the congress was opened, it was considered by Richelieu to be one of the most crucial elements in ensuring that French security would be preserved after the conclusion of a peace, not least because of the dimensions and multitude of interlocking conflicts characterising the Thirty Years War. According to his early conception of the securing or safeguarding of the peace, two leagues were to be established for Italy and Germany, whereby all contracting parties would immediately enforce the peace terms collectively if a breach had taken place. Richelieu therefore envisioned a system of collective security for Europe.[43] Under Mazarin, this conception of guaranteeing the peace was retained, and although the solution adopted was slightly different, the key notion that each party should mutually and reciprocally guarantee every treaty term was achieved.[44] The reason France pushed so emphatically for a mutual guarantee was that its leading statesmen mistrusted Spain (and, to a lesser extent, the Emperor) so deeply that they feared having to face them alone in case of the expected post-war Habsburg attempt at revanchism.

There were considerable disagreements over who the guarantors should be. According to the initial Swedish proposal of 1644, the guarantors would be able to immediately intervene militarily if a breach of the treaty terms was believed to have occurred, but the proposed guarantors would be limited to France, Sweden and their allies among the German princes—which would have rendered the guarantor powers largely Protestant. France on the other hand wanted all signatories of the eventual treaties to be granted guarantor status in order to further the goal of a system of collective security. The Emperor found it hard to accept the French and Swedish demands that the Imperial Estates—the Emperor's subjects—be included as guarantors.[45] However, the Emperor was not opposed to the guarantee in principle—indeed, according to Vienna, its scope did not go far enough because of the omission of Habsburg Spain from the list of guarantors.[46]

The guarantee was also discussed extensively by the envoys of the Imperial Estates. Interestingly, many of the German princes were unenthusiastic about shouldering the international duties of becoming guarantors in their own right. Many of the Catholic princes and the Emperor were also reluctant to give the foreign crowns a legal title to intervene in the Empire as guardians of the Imperial constitution. The early signalling of France that it was determined to place the treaty under a general, mutual guarantee was crucial in persuading many of the smaller princes, especially the Protestants, that a settlement was viable, because it would help ensure that the Catholics and the Emperor would not renege on their confessional concessions.[47] For France, conversely, the guarantee ensured that a collective effort could be launched against the Emperor if he violated the non-assistance clause by giving aid to his Spanish cousins in the ongoing Franco-Spanish war. Both crowns saw their ability to safeguard princely liberties as enshrined at Westphalia, and the Imperial constitution in general, as essential to preventing the establishment of Habsburg absolutism in the Empire, the perceived threat of which had led to their interventions in this Imperial civil war in the first place.

Peace terms

The treaty of Münster between France and the Emperor and the Empire (i.e. Imperial Estates) (Instrumentum Pacis Monasteriensis, IPM), and the treaty of Osnabrück between Sweden and the Emperor and the Empire (Instrumentum Pacis Osnabrugensis, IPO) were both signed in Münster on 24 October 1648 and form a single peace settlement—the Peace of Westphalia. Many, but not all, sections are replicated verbatim in both treaties. A separate treaty, signed in Münster on 30 January 1648, made a peace settlement between Spain and the Netherlands. It is not technically part of the Peace of Westphalia, but it was negotiated at the same peace congress.

The Peace of Westphalia consisted of three main elements: a reformed Imperial constitution; related to this, a revamped religious settlement for the

Empire; and an international peace treaty. It was therefore a document of both international and constitutional law. The peace treaties reactivated the 'Eternal Territorial Peace' that had been proclaimed throughout the Empire in 1495. This affirmed the general principle of amnesty, restitution and oblivion (IPO II, III § 1–2/IPM § 2, 5–6). It was declared to be a Christian and a perpetual peace, which was also a novelty, because previous peace treaties usually set a time limit. It was also declared to be a perpetually valid fundamental constitutional law of the Empire (IPO XVII).

The rights of the Imperial Estates were listed and enshrined for the first time (IPO VIII). Their 'rights of territorial rule' were safeguarded, as was their right of participating in decisions on major Imperial policy areas, concluding alliances with other Imperial Estates and foreign powers, maintaining armies, waging war and making peace. On the other hand, their alliance-making capacity was limited by the caveat that alliances must not be directed against the Emperor, the Empire or the peace settlement.

The true diplomatic masterstroke of the peace settlement was its optimised religious constitution (IPO V, VII), which laid the foundation for an improved 'juridification' of sectarian conflict, especially because Calvinism was finally recognised as a third official confession. All other sects remained banned, but the Jews' existing special privileges, which had been enacted by the Emperors' grace, remained unaffected. Confessionally motivated violence between and within territories remained illegal. Sectarian hate speech and excessive criticism of the religious peace were to be banned. No one could be prevented from converting to one of the three confessions. No adherent of the three confessions could be excluded from civic offices and from guilds on the basis of religion, nor discriminated against in respect of education, marriage, burial and emigration. 1 January 1624 was selected as the benchmark date ('normative year') according to which confessional possessions, rights of public (demonstrative) worship and the confessional status of each territory were to be frozen in perpetuity. A graded form of toleration was applied to all adherents of the recognised confessions, based on the situation that had existed in the normative year. Those communities whose religion was the officially recognised confession of the territory in question according to the normative year possessed full rights of public worship (*exercitium publicum religionis*). Communities of an additional confession whose worship had been publicly or privately tolerated in 1624 would continue to be tolerated after 1648, and were entitled to employ preachers. Those whose confession had not existed in the territory in question in 1624 received the concession of the possibility of private worship in their homes. They 'shall in consequence of the said Peace be patiently suffer'd and tolerated, without any Hindrance or Impediment to attend their Devotions in their Houses and in private, with all the Liberty of Conscience, and without any Inquisition or Trouble ... or [to] send their Children to foreign Schools of their Religion'.[48] However, these subjects enjoying this *devotio domestica* could be expelled to another territory by their territorial prince after a grace period of three to five years. This did not mean that the expelling government could seize any of the expelled subjects' property. Indeed, the subjects in question had the right to sell their property, or to have it managed by administrators, and were not to be denied official references attesting their qualifications and skills. They were permitted to return regularly to their home territory to inspect property, collect debts and litigate. Although the princely Right of Reformation was reaffirmed for secular princes, this now largely became a private matter for the prince in question. The confessional rights of his subjects would no longer be affected by a princely conversion.

In addition to these generally applicable terms, a range of specific regulations applicable to particular cases made the settlement more likely to be accepted and enforced as a whole. These included sharing arrangements for confessionally mixed Imperial cities such as Augsburg, the assignment of a different normative year to the Palatinate (1618), and an arrangement for the government of the prince-bishopric of Osnabrück, whereby an elected Catholic prince-bishop would alternate with an appointed administrator from the house of Braunschweig-Lüneburg (Hanover).[49] Most importantly, the normative year and other subjects' individual confessional rights did not apply to the Emperor's hereditary lands. Here the Right of Reformation remained in its unfettered form (except for some minor concessions in Silesia and Lower Austria).

These provisions mainly affected conditions within the individual territories. At the level of the Empire as a whole, the principle of full equality (parity) between Catholicism and Protestantism (including Lutheranism and Calvinism) was enshrined. This meant that majority voting at the Imperial Diet and the circle diets was no longer possible in religious matters. In such cases the representatives of the Imperial Estates would separate into their confessional parties (*itio in partes*) and reach an amicable settlement (*amicabilis composition*) through direct negotiations. One of the Protestants' chief grievances about being outvoted by the Catholic majority was therefore addressed. The Imperial Diet became the guarantor of the religious peace and the decisive instance in case of disputes. Protestant representation was stipulated for both of the supreme judicial tribunals of the Empire: six judges in the Imperial Aulic Council in Vienna (whose unanimous vote functioned as a veto in religious matters) and 49 out of 100 in the Imperial Cameral Court in Speyer. Similar arrangements of parity (or near parity) were made for other Imperial institutions, including Imperial deputations and Imperial commissions. The Ecclesiastical Reservation was retained, but now also subjected to the principle of parity. It therefore also guaranteed the perpetual Protestant status of the handful of Protestant ecclesiastical territories (Lübeck, Gandersheim, Herford and the alternating status of Osnabrück), in addition to guaranteeing the perpetual status of the more numerous Catholic ones.

The territorial changes effected at Westphalia mostly fell under the rubric of 'satisfaction' (with regard to France and Sweden and their ally Hessen-Kassel) and 'restitution' (with regard to most Imperial Estates). In the separate Spanish–Dutch peace of Münster (January 1648), Spain acknowledged the independence and sovereignty of the Dutch Republic, but held on to the Southern Netherlands (Flanders and Wallonia). Sweden gained Western Pomerania and the secularised bishoprics of Bremen and Verden as Imperial Estates, along with the attendant votes at the Imperial Diet, but also subject to the feudal and judicial overlordship of the Emperor (IPO X, XI). Sweden was granted 5 million Reichstaler for 'military satisfaction' (IPO XVI § 8). The complicated terms detailing France's acquisition of rights boiled down to overlordship and rule over almost the entire Alsace, as well as access rights to garrison key fortresses on the eastern bank of the Rhine (IPM § 69–91). One of the key threads running through most of the war, the Palatine question, was treated in IPO IV § 2–19 and IPM § 10–23. Bavaria retained the hereditary possession of the Upper Palatinate and of the original Palatine electoral dignity, thus remaining the highest ranking secular electorate. The son of the Elector Palatine Frederick V (the 'Winter King') was restored to the Lower Palatinate and was given a newly created, eighth electoral dignity. The Swiss Confederation was granted exemption from Imperial duties and from the jurisdiction of the Imperial judiciary (IPO VI). Arguably the most important stipulation of the 'international terms' was the non-assistance clause, according to which the Emperor was forbidden to assist Spain, either as head of the Austrian House of Habsburg or as Emperor (IPM § 3).

The guarantee clauses (IPO XVII § 4–5/IPM § 115–16) bridged international and Imperial-constitutional law. They stated that each contracting party, namely, France, Sweden, the Emperor and the Empire (in other words the Imperial Estates), was obliged as a guarantor to uphold each and every aspect of the peace settlement, even those that did not directly affect them. Before the guarantee could be exercised by force, the offended or injured party would need to seek redress through amicable settlement or litigation, and to wait three years before calling upon the guarantors to exercise the guarantee. The Emperor managed to insert the three-year waiting period, expecting this would ensure that most of the anticipated disputes over Westphalian terms within the Empire would be litigated at the Imperial courts under his judicial authority in the first instance.

Impact

Out of the five major interconnected sets of conflicts which the congress of Westphalia set out to resolve (the war between France and Spain; the war between the Dutch Republic and Spain; the conflict between France and the Emperor together with some of the Imperial Estates; the conflict between Sweden and the Emperor together with some of the Imperial Estates; and the Imperial civil war), it only failed to end one. Westphalia did not achieve the universal peace that had been its aim, but it did end the war in and for the Empire, and pacified central Europe, taking it out of ongoing geopolitical rivalry and defusing its potential as a geopolitical flashpoint for the time being. The mutual guarantee played a crucial role in this regard, because it secured both the internal arrangements of the Holy Roman Empire, which had caused the war, and the non-assistance clause, thereby shielding the Empire from renewed involvement in the Franco-Habsburg great power struggle.

The guarantee's rather impractical sequence of steps meant that it was never implemented in the manner exactly stipulated, but several de facto guarantor interventions were carried out, and its deterrent effect was considerable. It created a partial system of collective security, although not a universal one covering all of Christian Europe, as Richelieu had originally intended. Instead it encompassed only the signatories and applied mainly to the central European theatre. The mutuality and reciprocity of the guarantee of all clauses were an effective means of addressing the contracting parties' security fears of being attacked or undermined again post-war, at a time when mutual trust was lacking.

As was the case with almost all aspects of the Westphalian peace, it was a geopolitical compromise settlement. It would no longer be possible to transform the Empire into a more centralised Imperial monarchy capable of external power projection and aggression, as the Emperor at times appeared poised to do during the Thirty Years War. By acquiring Alsace, the French succeeded in blocking the Spanish Road. The foreign crowns' security interests were also safeguarded by their acquisition of territorial bridgeheads in Germany, by the separation of the Austrian from the Spanish Habsburgs, and by the defence of German princely and Protestant liberties, and thereby also the decentralised constitutional structure of the Empire. This all would prevent the emergence of a strong monarchy which would upset the balance of power and threaten French and Swedish security. Crucially, as guarantors, France and Sweden secured the right to police and, if need be, intervene in order to uphold the whole settlement in all its constituent elements: the decentralised constitution, the defence of their territorial acquisitions, and the enforcement of the separation of the two Habsburg lines. The nexus between these elements was summed up by the Swedish negotiator Salvius, who remarked that 'the Baltic sea will be the ditch, Pomerania and Mecklenburg will serve as counter-scarp, and the other Imperial estates will be, so to speak, the outer works' of Swedish security. The Swedish chancellor explained further that his aim was 'to restore German liberties ... and in this manner to conserve the equilibrium of all Europe'.[50] The link made between domestic liberty, the balance of power and the right to intervene could not have been set out more clearly.

Yet, contrary to the Westphalian myth, the Empire was not replaced by hundreds of independent sovereign states in 1648. It remained a mixed monarchy in which power was shared between the Emperor and the Imperial Estates.[51] The Emperor's constitutional rights were not subject to negotiation at Westphalia and were only indirectly curtailed by specifying princely prerogatives. This gave the Emperor considerable leeway to take advantage of his prerogatives and formed the basis of the revival of the emperorship in the later seventeenth century under Leopold I.[52] Preventing the Empire from collapsing into a weak confederation, and instead retaining its statehood in the form of a defensive association, also served a geopolitical purpose of maintaining the peace and the confessional balance within Germany. While Westphalia did confirm the princes' right to conclude alliances and maintain armies (subject to the caveat that these must not be directed against the Emperor and Empire), thus ensuring that the Empire would remain a decentralised polity, the prerogatives granted to the princes in 1648 were essentially just reconfirmed customary rights that had existed long before the war. The princes remained subject to the judicial and feudal authority of the Emperor.

But in some ways Westphalia reduced the princes' freedom to rule as they wished and increased the scope for supervision of, and intervention in, their domestic affairs. Firstly, the normative year greatly hollowed out the princes' authority over their subjects in confessional affairs, and their right to impose their own faith on subjects of a different religion was effectively abolished. Secondly, the Imperial judiciary, which retained jurisdiction between *and within* princely territories, and to which subjects could appeal by suing their governments, was made more effective and furnished with greater legitimacy at Westphalia, by the provision for near-equal Protestant representation in the two supreme courts. Thereby Westphalia strengthened the pre-existing judicial mechanisms through which legal interventions could be carried out, sometimes militarily, against princes who violated the rights of their subjects, their fellow princes or Imperial law in general. Westphalia also increased the scope of rights that could be defended by such interventions, by adding a catalogue of confessional and other rights. Therefore, instead of Westphalian sovereignty, it is more apt to speak of a system of conditional sovereignty or, more accurately, conditional rights of territorial rule on the part of the princes.

While the princes were certainly not sovereign, Westphalia also underlined the lack of sovereignty of the Empire as a whole, for the simple reason that a multilateral international peace congress was not only working towards peace terms, but also determining the constitutional set-up of the Empire—foreign powers intimately involved in making domestic laws being the antithesis of sovereignty.[53] This limitation of sovereignty was also evident in the guarantee of Westphalia, because it gave France and Sweden the authority to intervene in the domestic affairs of the Empire and its territories to enforce the treaty stipulations. It therefore tied the domestic religious-constitutional set-up of the Empire to an enforcement mechanism under international law.

Contrary to the conventional view of the role of Westphalia in the history of international law, it was not a fundamental basic law of Europe. However, it was a seminal event in the development of the law of nations. The instrument of the multilateral congress was adopted to negotiate peace after many subsequent European wars, and many of the solutions and methods adopted by the negotiators at Westphalia served as a model for later generations of diplomats. The use of the instrument of the congress reached a peak in the early eighteenth century, when congresses were convened (at Brunswick, Cambrai and Soissons in the 1710s and 1720s) to defuse international tension, resolve limited conflicts, and prevent existing conflicts from escalating into large-scale wars. A congress for similar purposes would be useful for the contemporary Middle East, as large-scale state-on-state wars have not occurred in the region. Although Westphalia inaugurated a secular order neither for the Empire nor for European international relations, it did include the assertion of the primacy of secular law over religious canon law, as part of its pre-emptive dismissal of a Papal protest or any protest against the Peace on the basis of religious law. This stipulation was seminal and contributed to the long-term secularisation of the basis of European international relations and law. Westphalia also left a clear imprint on subsequent treaty law, as a basic instance that was continually mentioned in subsequent treaty texts, as a 'reference peace', and as a basic order that subsequent treaties sought to reaffirm and re-establish. It was specifically the guarantee which largely ensured that the treaty's immediate legal effects had a broader European scope. For it was precisely in their capacity as *guarantors* of the peace that the signatories referred back to Westphalia and its guarantee when they concluded subsequent peace treaties, especially those involving the Empire. This was the case, for example, in the treaties of Nijmegen in 1679, Ryswick in 1697, Rastatt in 1714, and Teschen in 1779. Through these references, the basic order of Westphalia was reaffirmed by its guarantors as the 'foundation', 'fundamental norm' or 'unchangeable basis' of relations among them and within the Empire, following a temporary suspension during the preceding wars. Taking a longer-term perspective, it can plausibly be argued that by placing the confessional rights of religious groups under international guarantee, the Peace of Westphalia and its guarantee clauses helped to establish the principle of internationally guaranteed minority rights as a part of the positive law of nations.[54]

Contrary to what is sometimes claimed, the mutual guarantee did have an important practical effect in subsequent international relations. During the first two decades after 1648, the Imperial Estates perceived the Emperor as the greatest threat to the peace in the Empire, on account of his covert attempts at aiding his Spanish relatives in their ongoing war against France, and because of his perceived attempts at reasserting a dominant position in the Empire. For this purpose, a cross-confessional grouping of activist princes under the leadership of the archbishop-elector of Mainz acted as a continuation of the Third Party of the Westphalian congress, and concluded the Rhenish alliance with both 'external' guarantors, France and Sweden, while excluding the Emperor. The princes along the Rhine were particularly concerned that Austrian help for Spain could spread disturbances to their territories and suck the Empire back into war. This explains why the Rhenish mutual defence alliance grounded itself so consciously in the Peace of Westphalia, and particularly in its guarantee clauses, which were to ensure that its peace-conserving terms were adhered to and enforced with the help of the external crowns. The treaty text stated that the alliance was conceived as a measure to ensure the implementation of 'the general guarantee as instructed by the Peace of Westphalia, for the maintenance of peace'. The alliance, and especially the inclusion of France as a guarantor, did indeed have a pacifying and stabilising effect in the west of the Empire. It isolated Spain (particularly in the Southern Netherlands), and its existence probably deterred the Emperor from giving the Spanish any meaningful assistance and thereby kept his conduct within the bounds of his treaty obligations.[55]

Following the assumption of personal rule by King Louis XIV, France shifted its policy from keeping alleged Imperial despotism and aspirations of universal monarchy in check by defending the rights of the princes, to achieving security through direct military conquest and annexation. This radically altered the Imperial Estates' threat perception. While Emperor Ferdinand III had been seen as a danger to the peace and to princely rights, his successor Leopold I was viewed as a protector, especially in the light of French aggression and because the new Emperor made an effort to remain within the bounds of the constitution and to respect Westphalian terms. Louis XIV's use of the Westphalian guarantee as a pretext for self-aggrandisement was met with considerable consternation in Germany, and pamphlets appeared at the time bearing such titles as 'Considerations on how both crowns France and Sweden favour highly disadvantageous things for the Empire under the pretext of the guarantee of Westphalia'.[56] While there was widespread awareness that Louis XIV was abusing the guarantee, this did not lead most observers to criticise the institution of the guarantee as a peacekeeping mechanism itself. Indeed, they viewed the collective effort launched by many of the other guarantors as the correct implementation of the guarantee's collective security mechanism, an argument that was emphasised in the Empire's war against France in 1689.[57]

Louis XIV's abuse of the guarantee did not permanently discredit it. Following his death, French policy towards the Empire largely returned to its previous mode of fastidiously observing Habsburg actions within the Empire, in order to be able to seize upon any perceived breaches of the constitution, so as to rally the princes against their Emperor and therefore deprive him of a strong support base in Germany. Numerous princes had no qualms about calling upon the guarantee when they believed their Westphalian rights were being violated by the Emperor, other princes or foreign crowns. During renewed confessional strife in 1719, the Protestant princes appealed to France for support in upholding Westphalian rights. In the context of the Emperor's deposition of the duke of Mecklenburg in 1728, various leading princes discussed an appeal to the guarantors to intervene against the Emperor in defence of princely liberties. These and other examples show that there was a belief that the guarantors performed an important function in the Imperial constitutional framework, namely the safeguarding of existing legal parameters and the protection of weaker members of the Empire, thereby complementing (or at times even replacing) the role of the Emperor in this regard.

It was not only princes who readily discussed requisitioning the guarantee. In 1707 the Swedes under Charles XII carried out a military intervention against the Emperor on behalf of the Westphalian rights of the Protestant subjects of Habsburg Silesia, in response to their repeated appeals to the new Swedish warrior-king. It was justified squarely in terms of Sweden's guarantor status. One contemporary governmental pamphlet noted that Sweden had acted 'out of the possessed guarantee of the Peace of Westphalia, and according to its instructions', adding that 'the Swedish crown, as a guarantor, remains authorised to intervene and intercede for the freedom of religion'.[58]

With the 'diplomatic revolution' of 1756, France and Austria became allies against the upstart Frederick II of Brandenburg-Prussia. Their war against him was justified as an activation of the Westphalian guarantee, because Frederick had pre-emptively invaded Saxony. For the major actors, this was less a purposeful implementation of Imperial and treaty law than a fortuitous convergence of the law with geopolitical interests. Yet for many of the Imperial Estates (especially the Catholics), Prussia's actions did appear menacing and outright criminal, a perfect case for the application of the guarantee. It turned out to be an almost textbook-case implementation of the guarantee. It is the only example of a multilateral execution of the guarantee by all guarantors—France, Sweden, the Emperor and the princes—against a repeat offender who, by launching unprovoked attacks within the Empire, was riding roughshod over the system of peaceful legality that characterised the Empire. The participation of France in the war against Prussia was justified explicitly on the basis of the guarantee of Westphalia, not the recently concluded Austro-French alliance. In 1756 Austria formally appealed to the external guarantors and requested their intervention, and in the following year the Imperial Diet voted to carry out an 'Imperial execution'—a kind of Imperial war—against Prussia. Sweden and France then announced that they would join the execution, thereby exercising the guarantee.

Within the Empire, Westphalia had the effect of recalibrating and optimising the constitution. Following the great reform period at the end of the fifteenth century, Westphalia marked the last major constitutional reform. That the Empire survived on this basis for another 150 years despite being a defensively oriented, decentralised polity in a more rapacious international environment, was not only thanks to its function as a geopolitical buffer and guarantor of the balance of power at the heart of Europe. It was also because of the highly effective and successful mechanisms of power-sharing established at Westphalia. In general, Westphalia had the effect of enshrining the rule of law as well as German liberties.[59] The power-sharing arrangements between Protestants and Catholics, between Emperor and princes, and between princes and subjects all fell under the rule of law and therefore strengthened and improved a pre-existing system of the 'juridification' of social, religious and political conflict. A plain indication of Westphalia's success is that there was no more confessionalised war within the Empire after 1648, whereas such conflicts did continue elsewhere in states which tried to enforce uniformity. The Empire, by contrast, accepted in two steps (1555 and 1648) that peaceful confessional coexistence, regulated in great detail so as to remove any pretext for war and placed under international guarantee, was the lesser of two evils. As a by-product of making arrangements for a compromise balance between the confessions, the peacemakers at Westphalia also took the step of enshrining (an admittedly incomplete form of) individual liberty of conscience.[60] Princely conversions theoretically no longer had the potential to cause major crises within territories and beyond. After the conversion of the Lutheran elector of Saxony to Catholicism in 1697, for example, his subjects could no longer be forced to convert along with him, and Saxony officially remained a Lutheran Imperial Estate. Religious conflicts that might well have led to war, such as the 1719 crisis centred on the Palatinate, were instead defused by legal and diplomatic means.[61] A statement issued at this time by the Protestant party at the Imperial Diet commented on the improvements that Westphalia brought to the Imperial constitution, arguing that 'the refusal of Territorial rulers to accept that other fellow states protect foreign inhabitants and subjects was one of the greatest causes which led to the wretched Thirty Years War. It is precisely this wound which has been healed by the Peace of Westphalia'.[62]

Leading writers and theorists of the seventeenth and eighteenth century, such as Gottfried Wilhelm Leibniz, Nicolaus Hieronymus Gundling and Johann Jacob Moser, held the Peace in very high regard, often referring to it as the 'palladium' of the Empire. Jean-Jacques Rousseau famously regarded the treaties of Westphalia as the basis of the European political system and argued that preservation of the order it had created for the Empire was crucial for the maintenance of the wider balance of power in Europe. The Abbé de Saint-Pierre went further in the early eighteenth century and saw in the post-Westphalian Holy Roman Empire a model for a perpetual peace in Europe.[63] What the present authors are proposing for the contemporary Middle East is perhaps only slightly less ambitious, but worth considering in the light of the successes of the Peace of Westphalia outlined in this chapter.

PART III

SOLUTIONS

5

PARALLELS AND ANALOGIES

The world changes, and people, too; nevertheless, nothing really new ever happens; people and centuries resemble each other closely.

Christina, Queen of Sweden[1]

Searching for peace in the Middle East is a noble cause. Studying historical peace-finding experiences, such as the experience of the Peace of Westphalia, is intellectually and politically stimulating. However, one of the problems facing our situation today is the lack of strategic vision for all players of the Middle East stage. The ... factors that made parties to the Westphalia conference concede to each other are absent from today's Middle East.

Prince Turki al-Faisal, chairman of the King Faisal Center for Research and Islamic Studies, Riyadh[2]

The preceding two chapters provided an overview of around two and a half centuries of European history, with a focus on the origins, causes, course and consequences of the Thirty Years War and the Peace of Westphalia at its final stage. The emphasis has been on the nature of security crises, particularly in the region of central Europe, and how these crises and conflicts were pacified. As discussed, the Peace of Westphalia was instrumental in the pacification of central Europe, and its terms formed a central pillar in the security architecture of numerous major actors of that region. The reason why a Westphalian peace is being proposed as a source of inspiration and lessons for peacemaking in the Middle East is the set of parallels and analogies that exist between the

Thirty Years War and early modern central Europe, on the one hand, and conflict in the Middle East, on the other. This chapter focuses in depth on these similarities and parallels, as identified by the experts and analysts present at the 'A Westphalia for the Middle East' workshops, before turning to the directly operational part of the book, the concrete lessons that can be learned from them for the benefit of defusing security crises in the contemporary Middle East. By then, the present-day relevance and usefulness of early modern European history will hopefully have become apparent.

Of course, we must recognise the differences that existed over time and space, and not overwork the analogies and parallels. The pitfalls of this kind of diachronic analysis and analogy include their often imprecise and rather abstract nature. The Holy Roman Empire was a unity with the Emperor at its apex with a history stretching back more than eight centuries. It had possessed an order of peaceful legality since 1495 that all German actors accepted in principle and wished to see re-established. This degree of normative cohesion and consensus is lacking in the Middle East, making the notion of adopting a 'Westphalia' for the region appear challenging. However, as many participants of the 'Westphalia for the Middle East' workshops pointed out, there are common traditions across the Middle East that can be built upon, such as the unifying factors of Islam, the awareness of a post-Ottoman space, and a long shared cultural heritage. There is no Empire and no Emperor, but possession of the Holy Places of Medina and Mecca and the leadership position of Saudi Arabia for Sunni Arabs do make an analogy, even if an imperfect one.

It was occasionally mentioned during the workshops that the Thirty Years War involved the direct military confrontation of the great powers in state-on-state wars, whereas this has not occurred in the Middle East. Indeed, the analogy with the Middle East is most persuasive for the period until the 1630s, when direct wars between the great powers replaced indirect proxy war. This does not imply that such a phase of destructive conflagration needs to take place in the Middle East before a settlement as all-encompassing as Westphalia can succeed in the region. Instead, we draw the parallel here between the negotiations which occurred in fits and starts throughout the Thirty Years War before the opening of the Westphalian congress (1619–43) and the similarly abortive sets of negotiations that have occurred recently in Astana, Sochi, Geneva and elsewhere. What all these talks, both during the Thirty Years War until 1643 and in the Middle East until now, have in common is that they failed to solve the security crises which affect their region and which cost millions of lives. What changed the peacemaking fortunes in

Europe from the early 1640s was the all-inclusive congress, which is—according to many of the regional workshop participants—what the Middle East needs as well. Therefore, the parallels that are drawn here not only compare events of individual Middle Eastern states with those of the Holy Roman Empire, but also compare events and developments that apply on a regional level, in this way treating the Middle East as a regional unity, because interlocking conflicts affected and affect both regions.

It must be pointed out that the comparisons we make are not entirely analytically consistent. In some examples, the Emperor is compared to the king of Saudi Arabia, while in others he is compared to President Assad, for example. Similarly, different kinds of rebellion during the Thirty Years War will be compared with the same Syrian rebellion. A high degree of analytical rigour—such as would avoid any inconsistencies—would not be necessary for the purpose of this undertaking, as we are mainly putting the spotlight on general parallels relating to typologies of conflict, the role of religion and conflict constellations. Nevertheless, for the purpose of making comparisons and drawing parallels, it makes most sense to generally conceive the levels of analogies as follows:

Early seventeenth-century Europe	*Early twenty-first-century Middle East*
Individual Imperial Estates (e.g. Bohemia, Saxony)	Individual Middle Eastern states (e.g. Syria, Yemen)
The Holy Roman Empire	The Middle East
Europe	The world

Structural parallels I: complexity and multiple typologies of conflict

One of the basic similarities in both cases under investigation is the concurrence and confluence of multiple typologies of conflicts. Both the Middle East in recent times and the Thirty Years War saw a combination or concurrence of state-on-state wars; internal rebellions; civil wars; proxy wars; external interventions in civil wars; state-building wars; struggles for greater political participation and freedom; religiously infused wars; and geopolitical conflicts driven by realpolitik. In the classical state-on-state wars of the nineteenth century, centrally organised unitary states fought each other in symmetrical conflicts. The wars that are becoming the dominant mode of conflict today—not only in the Middle East and North Africa, but also in the Sahel, parts of central Africa and the Ukraine—are seemingly reverting to the earlier mode of asymmetrical conflict that prevailed in central Europe in the late sixteenth century during the Dutch revolt, and in the early seventeenth century during the Bohemian revolt and the Thirty Years War which it ignited.[3] The geographical focus of both conflicts (Germany and the Middle East) was and is a strategically vital region, which cannot therefore be ignored by peripheral powers, not least due to its resources and the high risk of a spill-over effect from regional unrest. Barring a comprehensive peace settlement, the continued supply of arms and funds into the region by involved powers therefore was and is a near certainty.

Then, as again now, the conflicts were and are characterised by great complexity, with a multitude of numerous actors of varying status (state actors, non-state and sub-state actors) fighting along unclear, rapidly shifting and intersecting front lines, in asymmetrical conflicts. They are asymmetrical in the sense that non-state actors such as militia groups or mercenary forces fight great powers such as the United States and Russia now, or France and the Emperor then. The complexity is such that it would be hard—in either of the two cases at hand—succinctly to summarise the course of the conflict, list the main fighting entities involved, or indicate the main lines of conflict on a map. To do all of this in relation to the largest human conflict in history, the Second World War, would be considerably easier. The longevity of both sets of conflicts is related to the wars being largely self-sustaining. While the inflow of external funds and arms are of course crucial to both contexts, the nature of the conflict also has given many of the involved warlords, militias and military contractors a vested interest in continuing the fight. A strong disincentive to disarm exists in both cases, which also existed at the level of states: the Swedes, for example, were existentially dependent upon allowing their commanders and soldiers to continue living off the land in Germany, because they could no longer afford to pay salaries that were far in arrears. Many militias active in Syria are disinclined to lay down their arms for similar reasons.

A high degree of alliance fluidity, with rapidly shifting allegiances, contributes to the complexity of both sets of interpenetrating conflicts. Saxony, for example, fought alongside the Emperor in the early stages of the war, was later in a state of armed neutrality, and then fought together with Sweden against the Emperor in the early 1630s, before shifting positions again and aligning with the Emperor thereafter. The military contractor Ernst von Mansfeld also worked for several different masters over the course of his involvement, and the Imperial general and military contractor Albrecht von Wallenstein was suspected of being on the brink of turning over to the enemy, leading to his conviction at the Imperial Aulic Council and his subsequent killing in 1634. These were the early modern equivalents of the warlords of the failed states of the Middle East and North Africa. As was the case with Europe during the Thirty Years War, the Middle East now is rife with shifting loyalties and internecine conflicts, especially in Syria and Yemen, where the former President Ali Abdullah Saleh and forces loyal to him were initially aligned with the Saudis, switched to an alliance with his erstwhile enemies the Houthi rebels (at war with Saudi Arabia), then indicated that he was willing to move towards the Saudis again, before being killed for this by the Houthis in December 2017. In January 2018, southern separatists and the internationally recognised government of Hadi broke their alliance and started fighting each other in Aden, further complicating the alignments.[4]

What adds to the complexity in both cases is not just the number of actors or the confusing front lines, but also the absence of clearly demarcated coalitions. In the Middle East now, but also to some extent during the Thirty Years War, the ancient adage 'the enemy of my enemy is my friend' does not always hold true; more accurate would be 'the enemy of my enemy might very well still be my enemy'. Turkey is at war with the Syrian Kurds, who fight the Islamic State. Yet the Turks are also at war with the latter. The existence of a somewhat unique actor such as the Islamic State, which is ideologically compelled to be at war with almost all other actors, makes this especially true in the Middle East. But even disregarding the Islamic State, the picture is complicated by the fact that Turkey's second major intervention in the Syrian war, 'Operation Olive Branch' in January 2018, was an assault on the Kurdish People's Protection Units (YPG), which are informally allied to the United States. Yet the United States and Turkey are themselves allies as part of the NATO coalition. During the Thirty Years War, the Emperor received assistance in defeating the Palatinate and the Bohemian rebels from the elector of Saxony, who was himself at war with the Emperor during other periods of the conflict.[5]

Structural parallels II: contested sovereignty leading to civil war

In both the Middle East now and during the Thirty Years War, an important part of the impetus behind the conflict has been fighting over the religious and constitutional set-up of states that are often already weak—what would now be termed 'failed states'. In both sets of conflicts, the nature of sovereignty itself was contested. In the Thirty Years War, the location of sovereignty within the Holy Roman Empire was at stake, which took its expression in a struggle over competing visions of a two-fold constitutional balance between the Emperor and the Imperial Estates, on the one hand, and between the princes ruling the latter and the subjects or corporate groupings of subjects within these, on the other.[6] Similarly, in the Middle East, the Arab Spring was essentially a struggle between conflicting views of sovereignty: popular sovereignty as espoused by the rebels and demonstrators, on the one hand, and autocratic or monarchical regime sovereignty as defended at all costs by dictatorial republican governments and absolutist monarchies, on the other hand.

The course of the resulting conflicts, and their respective stages, are also similar in both cases. Fighting begins with a struggle for greater political freedom and participation by subject populations and corporate bodies within states, and for greater economic opportunities. In the Dutch rebellion from 1566 (triggering the Eighty Years War with Spain, which partially merged with the Thirty Years War), and in the Bohemian rebellion, the rebels were fighting their Habsburg rulers for the freedom to exercise their Protestant faith and for political independence. In the Arab Spring, which was the opening act to the current round of warfare and strife in the Middle East, citizens rebelled against dictatorial regimes for greater political freedom, an end to corruption and sectarian marginalisation, and for greater economic opportunities. Similarly, an important reason behind the Bohemian rebellion was the marginalisation of the Protestant nobility in terms of access to government employment, on the basis of their religion. Restrictive, narrow, sectional regimes of access to power thus drove unrest and rebellion both then and now.

Tyrannical rule was a contributing factor to the initial revolts of the Thirty Years War and the related Eighty Years War, just as it was the main factor behind the Arab revolts of 2011. Although conceptions of what constitutes just and legitimate government have naturally evolved over the course of the intervening centuries, the denial of rights and freedoms, however defined, was a key element of the perceived injustice that needed to be fought. While the tyranny of the likes of the Assad clan, Saddam Hussein and Muammar Gaddafi was objectively worse than the kind of tyranny that governments exercised in early modern Europe, the Holy Roman Empire was no stranger to petty (and more formidable) tyrants, both before and after the Peace of Westphalia. On a superficial level, Assad is reminiscent of one of these tyrants in the Empire, Duke Carl Leopold of Mecklenburg-Schwerin, albeit from a slightly later period. Both are and were the rulers of a strategically important state. Both are and were guilty of tyrannical rule and major crimes against their subjects.

Both were propped up by the Russians, whose forces have participated in the violent elimination of domestic opposition. And both have been targeted by external intervention. While Carl Leopold lost control over most of his duchy in 1719, and was finally deposed in 1728, Assad's future is unclear—although a similar fate is a possibility.

It could be argued that even though there were rebellions against rulers in both cases, the kinds of people rebelling against the Habsburgs in Bohemia and those rebelling in Syria were quite different. The Bohemian rebels were essentially members of the landed aristocratic elites, who themselves lorded over the majority population of peasants, and who held considerable local power. While the Bohemian territorial estates were rebelling against the Habsburg dynasty in 1618–20, many of the peasants of Bohemia were simultaneously rebelling against the nobility. There was therefore a 'double rebellion' in Bohemia at this early stage.[7] The noble territorial estates wished to achieve more power for themselves by replacing their monarch with a more pliable one who shared their faith. They therefore offered the crown to numerous foreign Protestant monarchs and princes.

The driving force behind the initial Syrian rebellion, on the other hand, was the dispossessed and powerless ordinary masses seeking democratisation. They did not wish to draw in a foreign figurehead as the Bohemians had. The Arab revolts aimed in many cases at overturning the system of rule, whereas the Bohemian rebels arguably wanted merely to adjust the existing system in their favour. This discrepancy is true to a degree, but a core aim of both rebellions was the assertion of greater political participation and freedom. Syria and other Arab states also experienced 'double rebellions' of sorts, in which some rebels were moderate Muslims seeking democratic reforms and others were radical Islamists seeking to establish a caliphate. There are some important examples from the Thirty Years War of rebellions by the lowest strata of society, which are more comparable in their composition to the Arab Spring rebels. In the summer of 1626, for example, the peasants of Upper Austria rebelled against the temporary rule of the Bavarians, which was seen as illegitimate (Ferdinand II had allowed the duke of Bavaria to administer those parts of Austria that Bavaria had reconquered for him in 1619–20 until repayment of expenses incurred).

The Upper Austrian popular revolt was brutally crushed, leading to the death of as many as twelve thousand peasants and city dwellers—comparable to Assad's treatment of his people. Such rebellions presented both considerable threats and opportunities to stakeholders in the vicinity. Thus, Ernst von

Mansfeld, who was in the service of the exiled elector Palatine and the Bohemian rebels, along with the prince of Transylvania (an Ottoman vassal), exploited the internal unrest in Austria in 1626 by making plans to attack the Habsburg hereditary lands. These plans were not realised, but Wallenstein was forced to expend considerable effort in order to deter the would-be assailants. The French and the Spanish were more successful in such endeavours and launched several armed interventions in support of popular revolts in each other's territories, with France supporting anti-Spanish revolts in Catalonia, Portugal and Naples, and Spain supporting the French nobility's rebellion during the Fronde.[8] Similarly, in the Middle East, Iran has accused its great rival, Saudi Arabia, of supporting popular anti-government demonstrations at the end of 2017; Saudi Arabia had earlier supported Sisi in Egypt, because Sisi was suppressing the Muslim Brotherhood. Both states (and others) also supported, or helped suppress, popular uprisings during the Arab Spring on the basis of whether they could thereby weaken each other's proxies.

Structural parallels III: sequences of escalation—proxy wars to direct intervention

The support given to uprisings points to another key structural feature of the wars in both the Middle East and seventeenth-century Europe, namely the ways in which these initial revolts developed into bigger wars. In both cases, there was and is an incremental widening and escalation of conflict through intervention. In the Netherlands and Bohemia, as well as in Syria and Yemen, hostilities began with internal rebellions, and then escalated into broader conflicts through the involvement of outside powers, starting with more or less clandestine proxy wars, before moving on to direct military intervention. Thus, the conflict which began with a local rebellion against the Spanish Habsburgs in the northern Netherlands, eventually drew in other powers, including England, France and the Palatinate. It then became intertwined with the Thirty Years War, with both sets of conflict being resolved at the congress of Westphalia. The rebellion against the Austrian Habsburgs in Bohemia at the outset of the Thirty Years War spread to the broader region, to become what was effectively a civil war of the Holy Roman Empire as a whole, in which numerous Imperial princes revolted against their Emperor. The war then became internationalised through successive interventions by Denmark (1625), Sweden (1630) and France (1635). Spain had already intervened at the outset.

In a similar fashion, the rebellions and civil wars in Syria and Yemen have in recent years exported instability while importing intervention. The year 2015 marked a major stage of internationalisation and escalation with the Russian intervention in Syria and the Saudi-led intervention against the Houthi rebels in Yemen, as well as a spate of terrorist attacks across the Middle East, Europe and Africa, which were in part planned and directed from the war zones of Syria, Iraq and elsewhere. The predictions that the Russians would encounter their own kind of Vietnam in Syria have been proven wrong. Russia is today one of the most important regional powers in Syria and, together with Iran, the most important pillar of support for Assad. The Saudis, on the other hand, have been increasingly bogged down in a quagmire without scoring successes in Yemen, partly due to over-reliance on high-tech air power, and a lack of reliable ground troops.

In both cases, the regional powers view the sponsoring of proxies as a less risky and costly alternative, or as a prelude to direct military intervention. Both sets of conflicts have seen the extensive use of mercenary armies. Yet during the Thirty Years War and in the contemporary Middle East, proxies are often hard to control. Many leading Americans have expressed serious concerns about the use of funds provided to rebel factions, for example. France had similar problems in the 1640s, when it was outraged that the large subsidies it was providing to Sweden to fight the Emperor were also being used to launch a new war against Denmark, which did not further French interests. This points to the fact that in both cases, interventions could have completely unintended and unpredictable consequences. Some of the proxies used by the United States to confront the Soviets in Afghanistan in the 1980s ended up attacking the Americans themselves later. The American intervention in Iraq was designed to overthrow the regime and democratise the country, secure possible stockpiles of weapons of mass destruction, and thereby enhance US security by removing a root cause of terrorism and deprive terrorists of a possible weapons supply. This effort notoriously backfired.

Similarly, Spain intervened in the Thirty Years War, both by providing large subsidies to the Emperor and by sending armies to Germany, in order to keep the Spanish Road in friendly hands, furnish the Emperor with a quick victory over his rebels, and consequently (it was hoped) receive his support against the Dutch in return. Spanish support did help the Emperor defeat his rebels, but it also contributed to him overreaching himself and thereby provoking huge counter-interventions by other major powers, which resulted in the loss of the Spanish Road and in Madrid being forced to recognise Dutch independence in 1648. Thus, despite successes along the way, victories were often flimsy in conflicts as complex and interwoven as the Thirty Years War and the Middle Eastern crisis. The Emperor achieved a string of victories in the 1620s, but these were 'borrowed' victories, which relied on Bavarian, Saxon and Spanish help, as well as that of private military contractors, and which therefore deprived the Emperor of the capacity to ensure that it could be a lasting victory. Assad's near victory over the rebels in Syria is very much 'borrowed' too, and his future depends largely on decisions made in Moscow and Tehran.

Interventions during the Thirty Years War were carried out from a mixture of motives: geo-strategic considerations guided by realpolitik; economic motives; humanitarian concerns and desires to protect oppressed subjects; and confessional solidarity in helping co-religionists assert their religious rights. The three major external interventions against the Emperor during the Thirty Years War—by Denmark, Sweden and France—were mainly driven by the security imperative of meeting a threat that was perceived to emanate from a strengthening of the Emperor's position. The interventions were therefore not altruistic or motivated by a legally purist desire to enforce the Imperial constitution. But, protecting the rights of oppressed Imperial Estates and Protestants in itself furthered the goal of empowering the checks and balances against the Emperor, thereby weakening his influence and dominance of the Empire. Similarly, by militarily supporting a rebellion by the Catholic majority population of the free state of Grisons in northern Italy against their Protestant rulers in 1620, Spain was protecting its co-religionists against a possible massacre. But this also served the geopolitical goal of securing access to an alternative route for the Spanish Road.[9] There was therefore a strong reinforcing synergy between the ideological-humanitarian and the self-interested impulse behind intervention. A comparable nexus of motivations underlies external interventions in the Middle East. Saudi Arabia, for example, might well wish to protect the Sunni majority in Syria from the violent excesses of the Assad regime. But by arming and supporting militias fighting Assad, the Saudis are simultaneously advancing their self-interested aim of attempting to shut out Iranian influence.

The flipside of external powers carrying out interventions in civil wars and domestic rebellions is the appeal for outside assistance made by rebelling subjects and other non-state actors within states. This occurred frequently during the Thirty Years War as well as in the Middle East and North Africa more recently. In 1631, for example, the Catholic electors of the Empire appealed to France for protection and asked the French king to defend the imperilled Catholic religion in the Empire. The Bohemian rebels had appealed for assistance throughout Protestant Europe at the beginning of the war. Around twenty years later the Catalans appealed for French support in their rebellion against Philip IV of Spain.[10] Similarly, in the recent Arab revolts, several appeals were made for external humanitarian intervention and protection. The Libyan and the Syrian rebels asked for the imposition of no-fly zones in order to curtail the murderous excesses of their governments. The failure of France to undertake effective measures to restrain its Swedish ally and provide security for the Catholic princes considerably damaged France's reputation among the Catholic Imperial Estates in the early 1630s. On the other hand, its direct intervention and the revival of the war after 1635—ostensibly to defend German liberties—were resented by many of the same Estates. In the contemporary world, great powers often suffer from a similar 'damned if you do, and damned if you don't' attitude whereby interventionism and non-interventionism are equally criticised. This is especially true with regard to the United States. Many Middle Easterners and commentators across the globe criticised the American intervention in Iraq in 2003, yet also criticised its failure to intervene against Assad in the Syrian war or on behalf of Bosnian Muslims in the 1990s.

In both cases, interventionism is often driven forward by exiles, who organise publicity campaigns and provide a cause around which sympathetic actors can rally.[11] Their existence and prominent activism keep the conflict alive, by providing a tangible cause to fight for. The large-scale dispossession of Bohemian and Protestant rebels and the exiling of the elector Palatine, and especially his unwillingness to negotiate a compromise in the 1620s, acted as an engine for ongoing war and war financing. Similarly, the energetic activities of the Syrian exiles have contributed to an ongoing supply of financial and military support into Syria to prolong the struggle against the government. Multi-generational communities of exiled Palestinian refugees have also contributed to the long-term prominence of the Palestinian issue. An egregious example is the Iranian exile cult group, the MKO (People's Mujahideen of Iran), which at various times appears to have had support from Israel's Mossad, and possibly from the United States also.[12]

Structural parallels IV: overarching great power rivalry and realpolitik

A discussion of external intervention leads to the next major structural parallel, namely the role of great power rivalry, which is usually the driving force behind such interventions. In early seventeenth-century central Europe, as in the early twenty-first century Middle East, conflicts which were originally concerned with local matters tend to fold into the broader overarching geopolitical rivalry and contest between regional powers: Iran and Saudi Arabia now; the House of Habsburg and France then. Great power rivalry becomes especially influential after state collapse has occurred. In the Middle East, local problems such as tribal conflicts in Yemen, or local problems with a strong regional dimension, such as the protests for greater political freedom across the Arab world, soon became overtaken by the overarching geopolitical theme of Iran–Saudi rivalry. This echoes the situation in early modern Europe. The conflict over the Bohemian rebellion and the subsequent Palatine question, which were local and Imperial crises relating to the internal affairs of the Habsburg hereditary lands and the Holy Roman Empire, soon became subsumed by the broader Franco-Habsburg contest.

The opportunities and threats that arise from the domestic unrest determine the response of the regional powers, and their decision to intervene was and is largely guided by a calculation of how one's position can be improved in relation to the regional rival. Rebellions and local conflicts could easily be exploited in order to improve one's geopolitical standing. Another example of a local crisis being overshadowed by great power rivalry in the Middle East is the unilaterally organised referendum on independence in Iraqi Kurdistan of September 2017. This ostensibly local crisis of national self-determination was almost immediately exploited by Iran to extend its influence. Its Revolutionary Guards and its Shia proxy militias helped the Iraqi government to suppress the results of the referendum and to conquer Kurdish-held territory, including the city of Kirkuk. This improved Iran's standing in Turkey, which is even more opposed to Kurdish independence, and gave it greater leverage in Iraq, by strengthening the Shia militias and further marginalising pro-Western elements in the Iraqi government.[13]

Iran's critics accuse it of exploiting such events and unrest along the Fertile Crescent in order to extend a land corridor towards the Mediterranean coast, physically linking it to its allies and proxies in Iraq, Syria and Lebanon, and providing a route to supply active war zones. The Spanish Road in Europe was similar. Rebellions and internal unrest do not affect only peripheral states, but also the major powers themselves. Thus, unrest occurred in Iran in 2009 and 2017, and in Saudi Arabia in 2011–12. Around the time of the Thirty Years War, rebellions against Habsburg rule occurred in Bohemia and Austria (1618–22), Catalonia and Portugal (1640s), as well as in France during a peasants' uprising (Croquant rebellions, 1620s–1630s), followed by a noble revolt (the Fronde, 1648–53). Competing regional powers, both in early modern Europe and in the contemporary Middle East, have often bypassed the government of the other and addressed the rival's subjects directly in the hope of fomenting opposition, an example of which occurred during the recent Iranian unrest in 2017, for example, when President Trump promised the protesters 'great support'.

Often the decision to intervene is a direct result of the perceived crossing of a geopolitical 'red line' by the regional rival. The Saudis' belief that Iran was supporting and arming the Houthi rebels, thereby extending the Iranian sphere of influence into Saudi Arabia's backyard, was clearly such a line and led to the launch of the Saudi-led intervention in 2015. Similarly, the appearance of Imperial and Catholic League troops in north Germany along the Baltic coast in the late 1620s amounted to the crossing of such a red line for Sweden, resulting in the intervention of 1630. Geopolitical competition has driven not only proxy wars and direct military interventions, but also other intrusive steps into other states' internal affairs, most spectacularly the detention of heads of foreign governments. The widely suspected Saudi detention and deposition of the Lebanese prime minister Hariri in 2017 was probably driven by a motivation relating to the Iran–Saudi rivalry (especially the dominant position of Iran-backed Hezbollah in Lebanon), a step that was reminiscent of Spain's arrest of the elector of Trier for being allied with France in 1635. The Spanish also imprisoned Prince Edward, the brother of King John IV of Portugal, whom Madrid regarded as a rebel against the Spanish throne.[14]

Structural parallels V: State-building wars and no declarations of war

Another possible structural parallel relates to the phenomenon of state-building wars. One historian has described the Thirty Years War as an accumulation of such conflicts.[15] The Islamic State phenomenon is a good example, as it was not simply an exercise in terrorism, but a failed state-building exercise.[16] Similarly, the Bohemian rebellion from 1618 can be interpreted as a failed attempt by the noble estates to erect a new state free from Habsburg control, one whose Protestant character would have been secured and whose monarchy would have been limited by its elective nature and the extensive enshrined rights of the territorial noble estates. On the other hand, the Islamic State is quite unique and perhaps unparalleled in early modern Europe, in terms of its apocalyptic barbarism and elevation of violence, genocide and destruction as ultimate symbolic goals.[17] The closest equivalent to this terror group in early modern Europe might be the radical Anabaptists, who temporarily took over Münster in 1534–5 and imposed a reign of terror. Both state-building exercises of the Bohemian estates and the Islamic State were defeated after about four years. Following the outbreak of the Bohemian rebellion in 1618, its main armies were defeated in 1620 at the battle of the White Mountain, and the remaining rebels were driven into exile by 1622. Following the Islamic State's seizure of large swathes of territory in early 2014, it was defeated in its de facto capital city of Raqqa in October 2017 by the Kurdish–Arab alliance of the Syrian Democratic Forces.

A final structural parallel can be drawn with regard to the absence of declarations of war. In the Middle East there is a high intensity of violence and conflict without official declarations of war. The situation during the Thirty Years War was similar. The Peace of Westphalia was a peace treaty among powers who had never declared war on each other.[18] The French declaration of war against Spain in 1635 was the only official declaration of war among the many sets of conflict in the Thirty Years War, as technically required by the law of nations, and this was the conflict which Westphalia failed to resolve.

The role of religion and sectarian animosity

The general view until about the 1970s was that wars relating to religion were a pre-modern phenomenon of the past. Such conclusions have proved to be premature, especially in the light of developments in the early twenty-first-century Middle East. This is another area in which the nature of conflict has seemingly reverted to older, pre-modern modes of sixteenth- and seventeenth-century Europe. At times sectarianism has exacerbated initially non-religious political and constitutional conflicts, while also taking on its own dynamic; at other times it has consciously been instrumentalised and tactically deployed in the context of realpolitik-driven great power competition.

There are differences in each context, of course. The religious schism in Europe was only a hundred years old by the time the Thirty Years War broke out, whereas it is of more ancient vintage in the Islamic world. In early modern Europe, as opposed to the Middle East, the confessional fault lines were more fluid, as princes often converted (regularly leading to crises before the Peace of Westphalia defused the conflict potential of such choices), as did clergymen, civil officials and military officers seeking more promising chances of employment, and ordinary subjects in general. In the context of the Thirty Years War, the great powers' incentive to confessionalise conflicts was less pronounced than it is in the contemporary Middle East, for the simple reason that the two main opposing power blocs adhered to the same religion in early modern Europe (the Habsburgs and France were both Catholic), whereas in the Middle East the two main regional powers are divided by religion as well as geopolitical interests. These two sets of opposition tend to reinforce each other. In the Middle East, local conflicts and tensions which had little to do with religion in the first place, such as tribal conflicts in Yemen, or the struggle for greater political freedom and participation in Syria, have become 'sectarianised' by the growing influence of Saudi–Iranian dualism as unrest develops. In the Thirty Years War, on the other hand, the initial local problems and conflicts within the Holy Roman Empire were more confessional in nature than the overarching great power struggles, whose influence increasingly overshadowed the local issues of the Empire, arguably contributing to the deconfessionalisation of the conflict over the course of the Thirty Years War.

As a power-political instrument, the Saudis have injected sectarianism through inflammatory rhetoric, both as a classical strategy of 'divide and rule' in its eastern provinces where there is a large Shia population, and in order to deprive the Iranians of a support base among Sunni entities and populations. The Iranians, on the other hand, can benefit from such sectarian tensions, as they may help to bind the numerous Shia militias, such as the Hashd al-Shaabi of Iraq, and governments in Syria, Iraq, Lebanon and possibly Yemen and Bahrain closer to its orbit of influence and power. That said, the overall balance between the sects, where Sunnis outnumber Shias by 85 per cent to 15 per cent (or more) worldwide, may induce a reverse effect, whereby isolated Shia groups are actually less inclined to appear to align with Iran, for fear of bringing down greater persecution on themselves. The Imperial Estates in the Holy Roman Empire were similarly caught between the great power interests of the Emperor on the one hand, and the French and Swedes on the other; in this case sectarianism was not as central, although it did play a role in the enmity between Sweden and the Emperor. Confessional disputes in the Empire were largely related to legalistic interpretations and the possession of property. A more elementary, visceral sectarian animosity also played a role, especially during Sweden's war against the Emperor, which Swedish propagandists sought to portray as a quest to save Protestantism, in spite of the scepticism of the Protestant princes who were supposedly being saved.

The use of the principle of majority rule to marginalise confessional minorities was an important feature in both the Catholics' outvoting of the Protestants in religious matters at the Imperial Diet, and in Nouri al-Maliki's

Iraq, heightening confessional tensions in both cases. Religion had and has a real material relevance as it determines access to power and positions in many cases, such as employment in the service of the Emperor or, more recently, in numerous restrictive sectional regimes in the Middle East. Restricting access to office on sectarian grounds contributed to both the Bohemian rebellion and to the al-Qaeda/Islamic State rebellion in Iraq. The conflict over religion therefore usually transcends theology.

How can one explain the return of religion and sectarianism as a major destabilising factor after a period of relative absence in the second half of the sixteenth century in central Europe and around the turn of the millennium in the Middle East? A possible reason for this is a reduction of the unifying effect of shared hostility towards a common enemy: Israel in the recent history of the Middle East, and the Ottoman Empire after the Long Turkish War of 1593–1606. This war had fostered a sense of Christian cross-confessional solidarity and patriotic sentiment in the Holy Roman Empire against the 'hereditary enemy of Christendom and of the German nation', which clearly outweighed confessional animosity between Catholic and Protestant Germans as an emotive force. In the Middle East, hostility towards the state of Israel was a similar unifying bracket for the region, which united both Sunni and Shia, both secular Arab nationalists and Arab monarchies as well as Islamists in a shared purpose, especially during the Arab–Israel wars of the 1940s–1970s. Following Egypt's and Jordan's conclusion of peace treaties with Israel (in 1979 and 1994 respectively), the Arab–Israeli problem has been less prominent in regional geopolitics, the occasional Palestinian intifada and Israeli–Hezbollah war notwithstanding. The Israeli question has no, or very little, bearing on the current round of Middle Eastern conflict erupting in the aftermath of the Arab Spring, and was also largely unrelated to the rise of al-Qaeda and the Islamic State. Although sporadic events such as the recent American recognition of the Israeli capital city tend to temporarily revive such shared hostility again, Israel as a potent, cross-confessional unifying factor has faded enormously. The extent to which the rise of sectarianism can be attributed to this is largely speculative, but the timing does lend credence to this theory, as does the timing of renewed confessional confrontation in the Empire following the conclusion of the Long Turkish War.[19]

One reflection of the growing mood of religious strife in both cases was and is the increasingly pervasive trend of demonstrative expressions of faith and the resurrection of dormant elements of sectarianism. In both cases this was often actively encouraged by governments. The Catholic reform movement and the Counter-Reformation were driven by religious orders such as the Jesuits, but were often actively supported by Catholic princes in the Empire. Similarly, in an effort to placate Islamist radicals and offset possible rebellions, the Saudis imposed rigorous Wahhabi practices and dress, while exporting radical doctrines of Sunni Islam through the funding of seminaries and other organisations. Thus Arabic-style religious dress has appeared in areas where it was previously unknown.[20]

In the Holy Roman Empire, the revival of the Catholic Corpus Christi procession was a similar reflection of growing confessionalisation. A prominent example was the crisis surrounding the procession in the Imperial city of Donauwörth in 1607. The fact that such demonstrative public rituals had largely become obsolete in previous decades, but were now being revived as a provocation to Protestant communities, was reflective of the growing confessional antagonism in the Empire at the beginning of the seventeenth century. In Donauwörth this time it was the Protestants who wished to assert the domination of the majority. Here, the Catholic monastery of the Holy Cross insisted on its right to conduct such a procession, which led the Protestant city government to ban the procession in 1605, and to use force when dispersing it the following year. This occurred in spite of the fact that the monastery's rights had been confirmed in a verdict by the Imperial Aulic Council, one of the Empire's two supreme courts—although one which many Protestants viewed as biased because it operated out of the Imperial palace in Vienna and was appointed and funded by the Emperor. As a result of the city council's actions, the Emperor placed it under the 'Imperial ban' and appointed the (Catholic) duke of Bavaria to execute the verdict against the city; in other words, Bavaria was mandated to intervene in Donauwörth in order to protect the monastery's rights. Matters came to a head when the duke of Bavaria exceeded his mandate and not only occupied the city, but annexed it outright.[21] Examples such as these can be instructive about contemporary patterns of escalation of tensions.

It would be remiss to characterise the Thirty Years War or the current Middle Eastern crisis as religious wars, because of the absence of full confessional solidarity and the greater importance of geopolitical and constitutional matters.[22] As the Swedish chancellor Axel Oxenstierna explained, the war was 'not so much a matter of religion, but rather of saving the public condition (*status publicus*), wherein religion is also comprehended'.[23] Religion was and is undeniably an important factor, although it is often difficult to isolate and determine just how important, because it is often so inextricably merged with other elements.

Civil–military relations

Other parallels include the tenuous civil–military relations in both cases. Multiple military coups in Egypt and Turkey attest to this in the Middle East.[24] In the Holy Roman Empire, Emperor Ferdinand II condemned his top military contractor and general, Wallenstein, resulting in his death. Often tensions arose between military contractors and their princely employers during the Thirty Years War, because the latter pressed for more offensive military tactics, while the former were reluctant to put their soldiers (i.e. their operating capital) into harm's way.[25] The relationship between the soldiery and ordinary people in the countryside, especially those living along roads and rivers, was also poor, largely because of repeated, and often arbitrary, confiscations and exactions involving beatings, rape and murder. The resulting starvation and disease are one of the chief factors behind the terrible civilian death toll of the war. Conditions in Syria and Yemen are comparable; here distinctions between civilians and combatants are similarly disregarded by soldiers and irregular fighters and of course terrorists, and often by military planners at higher levels too.

Monarchy and dynasty, Al-Saud and Habsburg

Another parallel is that in the Holy Roman Empire (and early modern Europe in general) and among Persian Gulf states of the Middle East, the dominant constitutional model was and is rule by hereditary monarchical dynasties. These have also seen their fair share of coups. Both the Habsburg dynasty in Austria and the Al-Thani dynasty in Qatar, for example, have experienced palace coups and power grabs, the most prominent recent example being that of Crown Prince Muhammad bin Salman in Saudi Arabia. Both among the Arab monarchies and the dynasties of early modern Europe, a certainty and stability in the line of succession increased the state's assertiveness and confidence because of the perceived reduced risk of a succession struggle. Muhammad bin Salman's aggressive and bold foreign policy is perhaps a reflection of this. The importance attached to monarchical and princely legitimacy is apparent in the case of the killing of Wallenstein, the great military contractor and Imperial general. In the period leading up to his condemnation by the Emperor, Wallenstein had provoked Ferdinand II's ire by swearing in his new soldiers with an oath of loyalty to himself and no longer to the Emperor. It was suspected in Vienna that he would soon defect to the anti-

Imperial side. Despite Wallenstein arguably being in a stronger position militarily than the Emperor, his condemnation produced rapid results: his army peeled away from him and he was soon killed.[26] Legitimacy on the basis of the monarchical dynasty and the office of the Emperor was therefore more powerful than raw military capabilities. The monarchies of the Middle East have exhibited a similar resilience and enjoyed a greater sense of legitimacy than their equally absolutist or dictatorial republican counterparts.[27]

In general, a parallel can be drawn between the Emperor and the king of Saudi Arabia. The Emperor's position at the apex of the Imperial hierarchy and as the highest-ranking secular ruler in Europe was uncontested. The leading position of the king of Saudi Arabia, on the other hand, is not without challenge, but his importance in the Islamic world as the uncontested custodian of the two Holy Mosques of Medina and Mecca puts him in a somewhat analogous position to that of the Emperor. Like the Emperor, the Saudi government has intervened in smaller territories and states (Bahrain and Qatar, for example), and has even deposed or contributed to the deposition of recalcitrant rulers, such as the president of Yemen and the prime minister of Lebanon (2012 and 2017 respectively). Compare this with the Emperor's removal of the dukes of Mecklenburg (in 1628 and again in 1728), the ruler of Hohenems-Vaduz, present-day Liechtenstein (in 1684), and the prince of Nassau-Siegen (1707), among others.

Refugees

Another similarity between the Thirty Years War and the current Middle Eastern conflicts is the existence of major refugee crises in both cases. In Lebanon approximately one in four people are refugees, and in Jordan the proportion is about one in five.[28] Many cities in the Holy Roman Empire took up a great number of refugees in proportion to the total population size, such as the town of Ulm, whose population of 15,000 took in 8,000 refugees in 1634.[29] Moreover, the resulting shifts in the religious balance often sparked unrest in previously quiet areas, a phenomenon we are seeing in the Middle East today as well.

Communications technologies

A further parallel is the role of new communications technologies. While the seeds of the Arab uprisings were sown elsewhere, user-generated content disseminated through social media platforms such as Facebook and Twitter on mobile internet devices played an enormous role in mobilising the protests. Similarly, the printing press was a relative innovation in the period leading up to the Thirty Years War. The preceding Reformation and its knock-on effects were in part driven forward by the dissemination of new ideas by print—including extreme ideas and depictions of atrocities. In the Middle East, hate speech on social media has been a key driving force behind growing sectarianism.[30] The Thirty Years War was the first major conflict to occur at a time of daily newspapers, which also had a considerable effect on the presentation of policy to the public. Most major actors during the Thirty Years War were keen to present their policy to the princely and the wider public sphere by a demonstrative adherence to prevailing norms, including one's own desire for peace and willingness to seek peace through dialogue. Public opinion mattered then, as it does now.[31] Even tyrants such as Bashar al-Assad feel compelled to present and justify policy to the broader public.

Atmospheric parallels

There are also similarities in the general parameter conditions affecting central Europe on the eve of the Thirty Years War and the early twenty-first-century Middle East. Both periods are ages of pervasive uncertainty. Both regions in those epochs experienced population growth, climate change (from around 1570 there was a Little Ice Age during which temperatures dropped markedly, leading to lowered agricultural output and potential famine), general economic crisis, and social tensions and divisions.[32] Many contemporaries interpreted the appearance of a great comet that was visible to the naked eye for almost three weeks in September 1618 as a portent of terrible catastrophes to come. A manifestation of the general gloomy atmosphere (and the search for scapegoats) in late sixteenth- and early seventeenth-century Europe was the rise in anti-Jewish pogroms and witchcraft persecutions, during which scores of innocent women and men were judicially (and extra-judicially) murdered. These were in part reactions to economic crises, social upheavals and a general fear of the loss of control. The parallels to such persecutions in the Middle East include the manifestation of social malaise through the lynching of people accused of sorcery, magic or blasphemy by enraged street mobs, as well as actual witchcraft trials under certain jurisdictions, including Saudi Arabia and the victimisation of minorities like the Copts in Egypt, other Christians, in Syria and Iraq for example, and the Yazidis.[33]

6

LESSONS FOR THE MIDDLE EAST

PEACEMAKING MECHANISMS, DIPLOMATIC TECHNIQUES AND A NEW REGIONAL ORDER

The Peace of Westphalia is not a blueprint for peace in the Middle East. But if we look closely enough, we will see that it does offer us a number of instruments, methods and ideas. It is up to us to identify these, to extract them, refine them and make use of them in our diplomacy today.

Frank-Walter Steinmeier, Federal foreign minister (currently president) of Germany and the Osnabrück Peace Forum, 12 July 2017[1]

The Thirty Years War provided a crucial lesson: a proxy war needs a proxy peace. Just as external powers upheld the Westphalian Peace after 1648, any sustainable peace agreement in Syria will depend on the willingness and ability of both Syrians and external actors to serve as guarantors for stability.

Staffan de Mistura, UN special envoy of the secretary general for Syria[2]

In the light of the analogies and parallels discussed in the preceding chapter, it is reasonable to suggest the lessons that can be drawn for the Middle East from the congress of Westphalia, which solved a set of conflicts and problems that were quite similar to the travails that the Middle East is undergoing now. The lessons posited here are the result of extensive discussions during the project workshops of 'A Westphalia for the Middle East', where it was suggested that one can distinguish between two main kinds of lessons, which will now be addressed in turn. First are the peacemaking tools: diplomatic techniques that have proved to be effective in facilitating and enabling an eventual peace treaty, whatever the treaty terms might be. This also includes, crucially, methods of securing the success and longevity of the peace in the future. Here an examination of the proceedings at the congress of Westphalia has much to offer. However, we can also learn what needs to be avoided and which aspects of diplomacy are indispensable from the shortcomings of the congress, the failed talks between France and Spain in particular. The second type of lesson is the instruments of peace: in other words, the treaty terms themselves. The workshop participants deemed the first category to be the most useful, because on the whole it was not considered helpful or viable to simply transfer treaty content wholesale from a different epoch and region. However, there are some treaty terms that warrant our attention, that we believe to be potentially transferable. One example of these is the stipulation for Sweden's 'military satisfaction', whereby the Empire agreed to pay the Swedish army off, so that it would leave Germany. Providing some similar form of compensation to former militia fighters after a peace settlement (though perhaps distasteful) might prove to be necessary in the Middle East.

One of the striking features of the Peace of Westphalia was its innovative character in many areas of international law. While the features that were innovative then (notably, the multilateral congress convened at two different locations, and the mutual guarantee) may no longer be wholly innovative if applied now, this does not detract from their potential value as peacemaking tools in the Middle East. The innovative character of what is being proposed by the 'Westphalia for the Middle East' project is that the congress is designed to end ongoing wars and proxy conflicts in the region, while simultaneously also defusing the cold wars of the region. It would therefore be a congress designed to produce a traditional peace treaty, while also constituting a comprehensive 'preventive peace' designed to forestall direct state-on-state conflict between Iran and Saudi Arabia in particular, by reordering the region in a fashion that represents a compromise between the main players' core interests. A Westphalia for the Middle East is, in short, a proposal for a holistic new regional order of peaceful legality, in addition to being a set of suggestions relating to good diplomatic practice and peacemaking. The duality of the approach derives from the double capacity of the Peace of Westphalia as both a peace treaty as the product of a multilateral congress and a new legal-political order for central Europe.

A recurring theme in the discussions during the 'Westphalia for the Middle East' workshops was the supposed lack of normative consensus in the Middle

East, in comparison to the Holy Roman Empire, which might make it difficult to create a new regional order along Westphalian lines. Prince Turki al-Faisal hinted at this during one of the events, when he stated 'the social, economic, political and religious factors that made parties to the Westphalia conference concede to each other are absent from today's Middle East. The absence of a dominant visionary player to lead, is a major obstacle to bring parties to grand peace in the region.'[3] While it is true that the members of the Empire were relatively more united than the various actors of the Middle East—there was an overall consensus in the Empire, including among Protestants, that the Imperial constitution was an order of peace and legality that needed to be re-established with the Emperor at the apex of the judicial-political hierarchy—the Middle East should not be regarded as a blank slate, either.

Many of the workshop participants stressed that there are common traditions and elements of a shared normative basis that can be built upon. Before 1918, all Arab states in the region along with Turkey were part of the Ottoman empire. The borders in the region, often dismissed as artificial colonial constructions, have proved remarkably resilient and in many cases often follow the boundaries of the old Ottoman provincial districts. Although the unities that bind the region together are today concealed or partially concealed by those that divide it (including, but not limited to, armed conflict, nation-state traditions, more or less artificial boundaries, the effects of sectarian rivalry within Islam, the expansion of extremist tendencies within Sunnism, other communitarian divisions, and the development of political Islam within the region), unifying factors within the Middle East are still important and are still strongly felt by many inhabitants of the region. The attachment that all stakeholders in Germany felt to the Holy Roman Empire demonstrates the importance of a shared institutional memory on which people across the region can draw. Prime among the unifying factors in the Middle East is of course Islam (just as Christianity was the chief factor uniting early modern Europeans), and this remains true despite the fact that sectarianism within Islam has also been a divisive factor. For the overwhelming majority of Muslims within the former Ottoman space of which we are speaking, Islam means Sunni Islam, with its unifying centres of Mecca and Medina.

But it is not just Islam. There are important shared traditions and shared memories of law, custom, folklore, music, literature, food and, of course, language. These are easy to overlook or forget in political or geopolitical discussions, but they are as important as they always have been in the everyday lives of ordinary people in the region, and should not be underestimated. They quickly emerge when people from the region come together, especially outside the region, and at such times it can be hard to understand why the divisions in the region have often been so bitter. We have seen this in our own workshops and seminars.

Some discussants argued that common norms ought to be encouraged in order to make an overall settlement more viable. Dealing collectively with transnational problems, such as the refugee crisis and other types of humanitarian fallout from the regional conflicts, the Kurdish question or terrorism, could help to foster regional connectivity and norms.[4] Such normative consensus would make it more plausible to contemplate applying Westphalia's political-constitutional and religious terms for the Holy Roman Empire to the Middle Eastern region as a whole. Several of the basic principles underpinning the political and religious terms of Westphalia were deemed by workshop participants to be worthy of discussion and possibly transferable to the Middle East. These will be addressed after discussing the general diplomatic and peacemaking lessons which the congress of Westphalia furnishes.

The analogy between the two epochs and periods which underpins all these lessons and proposals, naturally demands an imaginative leap, in the light of the intervening four centuries and contrasting political, socio-cultural and economic contexts. It should therefore be stressed that what is being suggested is less a blueprint to be imposed as an external model than a series of lessons and inspirations tailored to conditions in the region, with the specific terms determined by regional actors.

An inclusive congress

The chief lesson from an analysis of the Thirty Years War and the Peace of Westphalia, which is the central idea of the 'Westphalia for the Middle East' project, is the necessity of an inclusive peace congress. The congress should address regional security problems through a negotiated solution—harmonising the leading actors' security interests as far as possible—and be reached by the regional actors themselves, before it is guaranteed internationally.

The complexity and multi-layered nature of the conflicts in the Thirty Years War meant that attempts at solving parts of them individually failed—such as negotiations only for the Catholic powers in Cologne, or a settlement based on the Peace of Prague (1635), which included only the Emperor and the German princes without the external powers. One of the chief lessons that we established early on was that, as had been the case in early seventeenth-century

Europe, the range of conflicts and grievances in the Middle East now is too complex and interwoven to be successfully solved with piecemeal negotiations aimed at addressing individual territorial parts of the broader regional crisis. While it might be useful to start negotiations on Syria in the context of separate formats such as those at Astana, Sochi, Vienna and Geneva, they should in the end merge into one comprehensive peace congress. Otherwise it may not be possible to satisfy a multitude of other involved state and non-state actors. An inclusive peace congress that drew in all parties would be an important step towards a negotiated new security order for the region under regional and international guarantee, as was established at Westphalia.

Time and again over the course of the Thirty Years War it became apparent that negotiations or settlements aiming at a separate peace did not last. There were always some actors among those that had been excluded from the separate arrangements who felt passed over and wished to continue fighting, because the arrangements made by others did not correspond to their own conception of a *pax honesta*. A similar situation exists in the Middle East. Even if the most dynamic powers and driving forces in the Syria conflict—Iran, Turkey and Russia—negotiated a settlement, this would by no means guarantee that peace would come to that part of the region, as too many other actors and stakeholders would feel dissatisfied with the resulting settlement, not least because their voices would not have been heard during the negotiations. Furthermore, addressing only the Syria conflict would ignore the manifold ways in which it is tied up with a whole range of other conflicts and constellations in the region and beyond. When the congress of Westphalia was opened, it did not formally include the Imperial Estates, but only the Emperor and the European powers. This solution was unsatisfactory to France and Sweden, who wanted all their allies represented, and the congress was only able to make progress when all involved actors were admitted.

Westphalia teaches us that an all-inclusive congress has a better chance of securing the peace. A peace settlement reached at a congress at which all parties are represented, and at which a negotiated reconciliation and harmonisation of their interests takes place, is less likely to be broken at the nearest opportunity than a set of bilateral or sectional arrangements. The resulting peace is more secure because the negotiations are under general and public scrutiny. Furthermore, with all stakeholders having been heard and having been able to present their interests and participate in the negotiations, any individual actor would be more effectively deterred from reneging on the final agreement because any such move would arouse greater opposition among all the other participants.[5] Before the Westphalian congress was opened, the French premier, Cardinal Richelieu, had been the foremost proponent of such a 'universal peace' being negotiated at a 'universal congress', as he believed that only a peace concluded by all interested parties was truly secure and durable.[6] Of course, the Peace of Westphalia was not a truly universal peace, because the Franco-Spanish conflict continued. Moreover, the Spanish–Dutch peace treaty was signed early, at a time when all other sets of conflicts remained unsettled, without any certainty that they would eventually be settled.

But this does not detract from the achievements of the congress, which in two steps solved all the major sets of conflicts at the time bar one. The French in particular had wanted to achieve a universal peace, rather than a particular settlement just for Germany. Similarly, one could also aim for a neutralised Middle East which is taken out of international geopolitical competition while international rivalry continues elsewhere, just as the Franco-Spanish war continued until the Peace of the Pyrenees in 1659.

Inclusivity could mean confrontation with uncomfortable realities and loss of face. At Westphalia, the Papacy was participating in a conference at which heretics were represented, for example, and the Emperor had to countenance the admission of his subjects and vassals as negotiating parties at an international congress with the European great powers. In an inclusive congress for the Middle East, the various actors would similarly be obliged to leave their comfort zone. For example, Turkey and the PKK, Israel and Hezbollah, Saudi Arabia and the Houthi rebels, Iran and the Syrian rebels, the Syrian regime and the Americans, would all find themselves at the same congress while negotiating on a theoretically equal footing—though they would not necessarily need to agree to sit at the same negotiating table. One of the innovations at Westphalia was the convening of a single congress at two separate locations. By such means, or by an adept use of mediation, the most unpalatable encounters could be avoided, if necessary. While the congress should strive to be as all-inclusive as possible, certain actors that are absolutely irreconcilable or insufferable may be excluded from attending, such as the rebel exiles from the Habsburg hereditary lands then, or whatever remains of the Islamic State now. The example of the Westphalian congress also shows that its outcomes can be unpredictable, not least because of the multitude of different factors that influence its course, including the negotiating parties' foreign political conceptions, war aims, military developments, domestic politics, shifting alliances, diplomatic culture, and the personal qualities of the negotiating diplomats themselves.[7]

A peace of exhaustion?

The treaties of Westphalia are often erroneously portrayed as a peace of exhaustion, which could lead to the depressing conclusion that the Middle East must first go through further bouts of destructive warfare before a similar peace settlement can be achieved. Actually, the situation in the Middle East is more similar in this respect to the end stages of the Thirty Years War than might be thought. While many of the smaller players, primarily the Imperial Estates, had indeed reached a state of exhaustion and together became the most committed peace party, several of the larger powers were able to continue fighting, as the French and the Spanish did for another eleven years. Similarly, although many of the war-ravaged countries in the Middle East have reached a state of exhaustion, the conflict could continue almost perpetually with the potentially endless inflow of martial resources from external great powers, whose continued interest in the region can be assumed because of the geopolitical and economic salience of the region. Oil revenue could also be a factor in prolonging conflict in the region.

The lesson to be drawn here is that the bigger powers who have not yet reached a state of exhaustion (and probably will not for the foreseeable future) must nonetheless be included in the peace settlement. More fundamentally, the lesson is that diplomacy works, and steps towards an overall settlement must be undertaken sooner rather than later, even if there is not yet a catalogue of principles upon which all parties can agree.

But the timing of the peace initiative is important. While one must not necessarily wait until a stalemate has been reached, the two sides should be relatively evenly matched (or at least believe that they are), otherwise one side will continue to believe that it can achieve more through a continuation of war (or commencement in the case of a cold war that needs to be settled) than through a peace settlement. The failure of the Franco-Spanish peace at Münster, for example, can be explained in part by the fact that each side believes it would still be capable of defeating the other. France believed it could turn the tide against Spain despite domestic troubles, and Spain wished to exploit the beginnings of the Fronde rebellion, the French state's bankruptcy and the minority of King Louis XIV.[8]

Is a ceasefire necessary to start talking?

The Hamburg peace preliminaries of December 1641, which settled the form of the peace talks by stipulating that the congress should convene in

Osnabrück and Münster the following March, and that negotiations between the European powers should be mediated by third parties, did not arrange for any kind of ceasefire for the duration of the talks.[9] While there was the occasional truce, such as the six-month ceasefire in 1647 (the treaty of Ulm) between France, Sweden, and Hessen-Kassel, on the one hand, and Bavaria, Cologne and Mainz, on the other, there was no generally binding overall truce during the congress of Westphalia. In the Middle East, too, several short-term abortive ceasefires have been arranged despite overall conflict continuing.

The absence of a truce during the Westphalian congress certainly complicated matters and probably delayed the conclusion of the peace, because the negotiators were obliged to take the fluctuating military fortunes of the armies of their princes into account, and progress could be deliberately delayed in the hope of achieving one more victory which would improve their bargaining position. Thus, the Spanish negotiators obstructed further progress in the talks with France, and began to delay agreements on basic points in the summer of 1647, because a number of military successes had led them to believe that they should stall for time in order to await additional victories on the battlefield which would strengthen their bargaining power.[10] Although a truce is clearly a desirable condition for a peace congress to take place, the Westphalian example also shows that the absence of a ceasefire need not be a sine qua non for the commencement of negotiations. The peace talks in Geneva and Astana have similarly taken place despite ongoing hostilities.

Diplomacy and negotiations

One overarching lesson from the congress of Westphalia is the importance of actors being willing to adopt and discover innovative means of diplomacy in pursuit of peace. The willingness of the diplomats and negotiators at the Westphalian congress to be innovative and creative and to compromise was vital in contributing to the successful conclusion of the peace. Informal modes of communication were as important as formal ones among the congress diplomats, even possibly more important. Over the years these diplomats formed their own peace party and a shared community of fate with a strong desire to make progress and push their masters towards an accommodation. Negotiators for a Middle Eastern peace should similarly stay at the congress location and negotiate until they have thrashed out a settlement, even if this takes months or years, as happened in Münster and Osnabrück.

As with the Westphalian congress, the negotiators should be high-ranking politicians, officials or courtiers from their home governments and courts, equipped with broad plenipotentiary powers. They would need to be selected very carefully, with an important criterion being their personal philosophies and conceptions of peace along with their diplomatic and bargaining prowess. Research on the failure of the negotiations between France and Spain at the congress of Westphalia has shown that one of the reasons why peace was elusive was the personal animosity of the negotiators to the opposing state, which was deeply rooted and grounded in traditional national stereotypes and tropes.[11] More open-minded plenipotentiaries would need to be selected for a comprehensive Middle Eastern peace congress. An important reason for the success of the congress of Westphalia was the negotiators' willingness to be daring in their choice of interlocutors. Examples include the interconfessional conferences of moderates willing to compromise (the Third Party), while excluding the intransigent hardliners, and the Emperor agreeing to the participation of the Imperial Estates. Middle Eastern negotiators would need to be similarly willing to explore unknown diplomatic terrain, and to enter into talks with unpalatable opponents in pursuit of peace.

Westphalia also shows that mediators can be useful and need not even be neutral.[12] During the Franco-Spanish negotiations, the Dutch—allies of France and themselves at war with Spain—proved to be more effective mediators than the (formally) neutral Pope, precisely because they had more at stake themselves in the success of the negotiations than the more distant pontiff. Mediation by Denmark and Venice/the Papacy was settled before the congress at the Hamburg peace preliminaries, but the diplomats at Westphalia were flexible, and the envoys at Osnabrück soon realised that what appeared promising in theory could be less effective in practice. They therefore opted for direct negotiations between the parties. Another indication of their flexibility is that they did not insist on settling every single matter but instead focused on the most pressing points, while more minor ones were postponed and delegated to be treated at the subsequent Imperial Diet—the so-called *negotia remissa*. The fact that the negotiations took many years despite this points to the magnitude of the problems that were settled. A peace congress for the Middle East would do well to adopt a similar procedure in order to avoid encumbering its negotiations with unnecessary details.

Trust?

Several workshop participants of 'A Westphalia for the Middle East' noted that there is widespread and mutual lack of trust on the part of the main regional adversaries in the Middle East. At several points the historians present emphasised that this was true in Europe too at the outset of the Westphalian peace negotiations—and even beyond the end of them; there was little or no mutual trust. It was the major powers' signalling of their willingness to place the whole settlement under guarantee that encouraged a degree of confidence in the viability of the negotiations. Following the conclusion of the peace, it took about two generations for trust to be re-established in the Holy Roman Empire among Catholics and Protestants, slowly grown through peaceful coexistence. This is a vital and central lesson from Westphalia: the absence of trust should not prevent negotiations from getting started—the peace process itself has to generate trust, not the other way around.

That said, a minimum degree of trust in the opponent's readiness to adhere to a future treaty is necessary, although the mutual guarantee can mitigate against the lack even of that, as we shall argue. The importance of a minimum level of trust was demonstrated by the failure of the Franco-Spanish negotiations at Münster, which resulted in part from a mutual conviction that the opponent was absolutely untrustworthy. The main instructions for the French embassy at Westphalia stated, 'experience has taught us that the Spanish only adhere to treaties as long as they are useful to them, and will break them as soon as it is advantageous'.[13] The Middle East is in a relatively more fortuitous position with regard to a general peace, because no direct war between the two main regional adversaries, Iran and Saudi Arabia, has yet occurred, and this may make it easier to muster that lowest level of necessary trust.[14]

Transparency?

The parallel between the Thirty Years War and the Middle East leads to a further lesson, namely the more-or-less justified security fears about the opponent's suspected hegemonic goals. This fear of the other side exploiting one's own weakness in order to establish regional dominance, or what was then termed universal monarchy, afflicted the Habsburgs and France then, just as it stifles trust between Iran and Saudi Arabia now, and requires more effective perception management. The workshop participants of 'Westphalia for the Middle East' deemed this important because changing hostile perceptions might be more difficult than changing facts on the ground. So, for a mutually acceptable regional settlement to be reached, the workshop discussants concluded that the negotiating parties need to set out, openly and transparently, their core security interests at the outset, tied in to what each side considers to be its legitimate zone of influence. This occurred to a certain degree at the Peace of Westphalia with the 'peace propositions' that were exchanged at the outset.

But, as in many negotiations, there was no complete transparency at the outset at Münster and Osnabrück. Rather, negotiations began with each side presenting their maximum level of demands and minimum level of concessions, and it was important for each party to conceal the maximum level of concession that it was actually willing to make. This was similar to a game of poker in which each player tries to keep his cards as close to his chest as possible. Indeed, gambling metaphors were used frequently by the negotiators themselves.[15] It was to be expected that the negotiators would not always be entirely honest. Research has shown that the practice of 'dissimulation' during negotiations—concealing one's reasoning and goals—was widespread and even expected. Other common forms of disingenuous communication included reverse psychology and feigned ignorance, which could at times even accelerate agreement on individual points.[16] After a process of haggling the eventual terms were agreed. But it was important not to overplay one's hand: a reason for the collapse of the Franco-Spanish negotiations was the French practice of pressing excessively for unrealistic concessions, which the Spaniards were not willing to give.[17] It was only through drawn-out negotiations and haggling at the congress that the diplomats were able to discern the true extent of their adversaries' minimum demands and maximum concessions, making it possible to harmonise these.

At Osnabrück this process helped to achieve the religious settlements because it became clear over many months of talks that the Emperor was not as intransigent in confessional matters as had generally been assumed. Initially the Protestant Imperial Estates and the Swedes believed that the Emperor was following a hard line over the religious constitution of the Empire, but eventually it emerged that Ferdinand III was actually willing to make considerable concessions to Protestant rights in the Empire. He only remained uncompromising in his determination to keep his own hereditary lands of Austria and Bohemia completely Catholic with an unrestricted Right of Reformation.[18] This stance was one that most of the Protestants could work with, thus permitting the final compromise settlement. While the treaty terms in relation to the religious constitution of the Empire needed to be arranged in the greatest possible detail before it was acceptable to all sides, in other areas, such as the Alsace terms, ambiguities in the treaty text could help bring about the necessary consensus.[19]

At a future peace congress for the Middle East, one can therefore expect that discovering each side's true interests and the extent that they are willing to compromise will require not only transparency but also extended negotiations, during which the parties can thoroughly sound each other out. It would be helpful if states declared their vital interests clearly and openly over the course of the congress negotiations. They must also be willing, to a degree, to recognise the legitimate interests of others on a reciprocal basis, and, where necessary, to accept compromise when legitimate interests conflict.

Participants of the 'Westphalia for the Middle East' workshops discussed what the main actors' core interests might be. What is more important for the leading states in the region is less direct territorial expansion than maintaining their own perceived zones of informal influence. For Iran, prime interests include the removal of the US military threat, and the establishment of a regional security structure encompassing the Persian Gulf (including Iraq), Syria, and also Afghanistan and Pakistan. As for zones of influence, Iran is primarily concerned with its immediate neighbours; not Yemen or Libya, but Syria, Afghanistan, Iraq and possibly Lebanon. There is also a concern in Iran—both in government and among the people—that Israel is now manipulating Arab states to its own ends. Saudi Arabia's core interests were suggested as being the achievement of regional stability and removal of the Iranian threat. Yemen, the GCC states, Syria and Jordan would need to remain parts of the kingdom's zone of influence. The Saudis are also unwilling to accept that the self-defined interest of Iran should be allowed to override the wishes of the Syrian people. For Turkey, the prime concern is that no Kurdish state should emerge, especially in Syria, whether as such or in de facto form through arrangements for regional autonomy. But Turkey might be more relaxed about movements towards greater Kurdish autonomy in Iraq. Russia is probably looking for an exit strategy in Syria. It wants to retain control of the port at Tartus, and to have continuing oversight in the region, but also wants the fighting to be over and to have a stable settlement in place.

Workshop participants noted that the area of overlap or conflict between the stated interests of Iran and Saudi Arabia did not seem all that great. Both confirmed that their other interests were more pressing to them than Lebanon or the Palestinian issue, for example (for Iran it was more a question of influence than interest as such). It is possible that Iran's seeming ascendancy in its struggle for influence with Saudi Arabia might force a contraction of Saudi demands, despite vocal support from President Trump. Previously they had wanted confederation in Iraq and partition in Syria, but the latter at least seems no longer practicable. A parallel can be drawn here with the Emperor's abandonment of earlier maximalist demands at Westphalia. The UAE and Bahrain perhaps fear Iran more than Saudi Arabia does. They accuse Tehran of seeking to build a new empire, and of building its own security at the expense of the security of others, while sponsoring non-state actors and militias to do its bidding. Jordan, with an enormous refugee population, claims that a resolution of the Israeli–Palestinian question is an important interest. Egypt, traditionally a leading power in the region, has recently been reluctant to take a forward role in discussions of regional security, being preoccupied with internal problems. But the dictates of internal policy have, for example, brought Egypt closer to Saudi Arabia (against the Muslim Brotherhood) and have encouraged Egypt to side with Saudi Arabia against Qatar.

Interim settlements?

Developments during the Westphalian congress suggest further lessons for a hoped-for congress in the Middle East. The inclusivity of the congress and consequently the high number of participants meant that it was difficult to achieve the lowest level of necessary alignment of all the various sets of interests involved. This was shown by the lack of clear, unified policy objectives among allies. The two branches of the House of Habsburg, Spain and Austria, failed to arrange a unified policy stance towards their common adversary, France. Spain's adversaries, France and the Netherlands, also failed to pursue a unified policy direction towards their shared enemy, Spain, despite being allies. This is reflected in these two sets of allies' eventual decision to conclude a separate peace: the Emperor made peace with France, thereby abandoning his Spanish ally, and the Dutch made peace with Spain, abandoning their French ally. Even France and Sweden, whose alliance remained strong throughout the congress, and who made good on their reciprocal promise to desist from concluding a separate peace, had serious doubts and suspicions about each other during the negotiations, with France fearing that Sweden would unconditionally support the Protestants' religious demands, for example.

This leads to the question of whether insisting on an overall universal settlement that draws all actors into a single treaty or set of simultaneous treaties is necessarily a prudent approach for achieving peace. As argued above, an all-encompassing overall settlement would be the most desirable and secure form of peace for the Middle East, just as it had been the aim of the 'universal congress' of Westphalia when it was convened. Yet from the summer of 1647 it became increasingly apparent that the Franco-Spanish peace would be unattainable, while the Spanish–Dutch settlement increasingly appeared within grasp. According to the original conception of the universal peace, these two sets of conflicts would have to be settled along with those relating to France, Sweden and the Empire at the same time. But in the end, the French decided to continue negotiating despite having lost their Dutch ally at an earlier separate peace (January 1648), and the Emperor eventually relented and signed the peace treaties with France and Sweden in October 1648, even without the inclusion of Spain. The result was the pacification of central Europe, while the war between France and Spain in the west continued. The lesson is that although a 'grand bargain'—such as that which the congress of Westphalia was supposed to achieve—should be the aim for the Middle East, given the interlocking and interpenetrating nature of its various constituent conflicts, the parties must not indefinitely insist on it at the cost of lesser agreements. A degree of flexibility is desirable if it can generate peace for at least a substantial proportion of the area that is to be pacified.

The 'Third Party'

Chapter 4 related that the 'Third Party' of smaller actors, who had suffered most from the war and who were guided by an unconditional desire for peace, assumed the initiative when it became clear that France and Spain would not reach an agreement and that the congress was therefore threatened with dissolution. This informal grouping was unprecedented because it was cross-confessional and characterised by a mutual willingness to compromise. It signalled the end of automatic confessional solidarity and was held together solely by the aim of a lasting peace. By uniting in this fashion, the actors reached a critical mass which allowed them to force their more powerful allies to achieve an accommodation, or else risk isolation. They acted as an informal mediator between Sweden and the Emperor, who then agreed to a peace that did not include Spain, thereby ensuring that the war would no longer be fought in the Empire.[20]

During the workshops there was a considerable amount of discussion about the possibility of such a diplomatic technique in a congress for a Middle Eastern peace. It was agreed that such a third party should consist of powers that have a self-interest in peace by being directly affected, and would therefore not act as separated and neutral mediators would. They should be guided by the ultimate aim of peace and be willing to cooperate with anyone. They must be thick-skinned and able to ignore accusations of perfidy and betrayal by the uncompromising hardliners or by allies. They should also, however, carry enough clout—either in terms of geopolitical capabilities or in terms of legitimacy—to enable them to effectively apply pressure. But the discussants also recognised that the analogy was not straightforward, because the Third Party of the seventeenth century consisted of Imperial Estates, whose constitutional position helped them to put pressure on the Emperor within a framework that does not exist in the Middle East today. Whereas the idea that the EU or some of its member states could form such a Third Party seemed promising at first sight, as they are indirectly affected by the conflicts in the region in the form of terrorist attacks and the influx of refugees, further discussion suggested that Europe in fact lacked the political will and leverage to do so. Others argued that Middle Eastern states, whose lands and people have been laid to waste, and who have found themselves trapped between the regional powers, Saudi Arabia and Iran, should themselves form such a third party—though it was also recognised that they lacked the unity of the Westphalian Third Party. Regardless of who could constitute such a Third Party in a contemporary Middle Eastern peace congress, the lesson to draw is that despite the necessity of including the involved major powers in a congress, they need not necessarily be the driving force behind the peace initiatives and negotiations.

Securing the peace: the mutual guarantee

It is not enough for a peace settlement simply to be signed. There needs to be an assurance that the resulting peace is secured—in other words, that the conflicts ended by the treaty do not resume. This aim, *assecuratio pacis*, was a very important topic of negotiation at the Westphalian congress, and several tools were adopted to further this crucial goal.[21] The fact that the congress was as all-inclusive as possible itself ensured that it would be a secure peace, because no one would feel bypassed. A clause pre-emptively rejecting any protest against the settlement, on the basis of religious canon law or by the Pope, was also intended to secure the peace. Another useful feature was the stipulation that the whole settlement should remain valid for all participating parties, even for those who protested against individual terms or the whole peace itself, as well as those who refused to sign. Dispensing with a requirement for unanimous agreement was essential. Another transferable mechanism could be to convene a second follow-up conference to arrange all the details of how the peace terms will be implemented, as occurred at the Nuremberg Execution Diet in 1649–50.[22] This would ensure that the main peace congress can focus on matters of principle and that the agenda is not overloaded with details of policy implementation. It should also make sure that the peace terms are actually executed.

The most important tool of securing the peace, however, was its mutual guarantee, described by one of the participating historians of the 'Westphalia for the Middle East' workshops as the 'centrepiece' of the whole peace settlement.[23] The success of the Westphalian guarantee was based on the inclusion of all involved actors as guarantors, whereby warring parties became guarantors of their own peace after the conclusion of the peace settlement. As Staffan de Mistura, the UN special envoy for Syria, noted at one of the workshops, 'The Thirty Years War provided a crucial lesson: a proxy war needs a proxy peace. Just as external powers upheld the Westphalian Peace after 1648, any sustainable peace agreement in Syria will depend on the willingness and ability of both Syrians and external actors to serve as guarantors for stability.'[24] Fundamentally, a mutual guarantee of a negotiated settlement ensures that the peace is secure despite mutual mistrust, because each contracting party's vital interests are woven somewhere into the treaty in such a way as to give them good reason to uphold the peace settlement in its entirety. The mutuality and reciprocity of the guarantee of all clauses is therefore an effective means of addressing the contracting parties' security fears for the period after the signature of the treaty.

Treaties had been guaranteed in the past, but according to early modern theories of the law of nature and nations, guarantors should be powerful non-involved third parties, usually mediators, or higher-ranking persons such as the Pope. The Westphalian guarantee was innovative in the sense that this was the first time that the warring parties and contracting signatories themselves became the guarantors of their own peace settlement in a mutual and reciprocal set-up. Also, the solution adopted at Westphalia provided not only for powerful, non-neutral guarantors (France, Sweden and the Emperor), but also weaker non-neutral ones, namely the German princes, who had been most severely affected by the war. Because each signatory was also a guarantor, strictly speaking there were no 'external' guarantors supervising adherence to the settlement by the contracting parties. Instead, each contracting party as a guarantor pledged to defend and uphold—by armed force if necessary—every aspect of the peace treaty, even those that did not affect them individually.

This amounted to a collective security system for central Europe among the contracting parties of the treaty. If one were to draw lessons for today's Middle

East, it would make sense to conceive of internal and external guarantors as comparable now to regional (Middle Eastern) and international (global) guarantors. This is because, in addition to being an international peace treaty, Westphalia was also a fundamental constitutional law for the Holy Roman Empire. It makes sense to think of the Emperor and the German princes as the internal guarantors, while France and Sweden were the external ones, despite the fact that they were also themselves contracting parties. But most of the political-constitutional terms of the peace did not apply to them—only to the neutralised zone of the Empire.

In addition to being innovative, the guarantee was also successful because the negotiating parties knew that it was on the agenda and would likely be adopted as a means of securing the peace, and this was a key factor in persuading them to negotiate in the first place and then also to actually sign the peace treaty. The fact that the external powers, especially France, had signalled early on that they attached great importance to such a guarantee helped persuade the smaller actors, particularly the Protestant princes, that the settlement as a whole was viable. In the context of the absence of trust, many Protestants suspected that the Emperor and the Catholics would resume confessional depredations after the withdrawal of foreign armies from Germany. But with the prospect of the guarantee, they received assurance that the French (or the Swedes) would march back into Germany to prevent this. Furthermore, the knowledge that the Emperor was signing an agreement which gave the external crowns a legitimate legal title to intervene in such cases was believed to act as a deterrent against breaches of the peace, fostering trust in the mechanisms of peace conservation. France, on the other hand, gained assurance that a collective effort could be launched by all the parties against the Habsburg Emperor if he helped Habsburg Spain in the ongoing Franco-Spanish war in violation of treaty stipulations.

Participants at the workshops recognised that local, regional actors themselves need similarly to guarantee their own peace settlement, as they would be most interested in upholding its terms and securing the peace in their region. The lesson is that guarantors need to be powerful enough to enforce the provisions, and not uninterested to an extent that prevents them from intervening in the case of treaty breach. In other words, a guarantor's capacity and readiness to intervene need to be credible. Potential abuse and hegemony by a powerful guarantor can be offset by designating mutually balancing guarantors, just as France balanced Emperor Ferdinand III during his alleged revanchism after the conclusion of the peace, and Emperor Leopold I then balanced Louis XIV's aggression and abuse of the guarantee. There was a general agreement that Saudi Arabia, Iran, Turkey and Egypt would need to form the core of a regional guarantee structure. There was also discussion of the important role that Jordan might have, especially in southern Syria, while some argued that Russia should be considered a regional rather than an international actor. Regarding the role of the regional guarantors, it was argued that they would be tasked with enforcing the treaty terms and, more broadly, securing the peace, especially in the light of the anticipated continued existence of numerous militias, ensuring the integrity of existing borders, providing assistance in the rebuilding of more inclusive regimes, and protecting the rights of minorities within states.

The Middle East has perhaps been too inclined to look to outsiders to make and guarantee peace single-handedly. Therefore, while regional actors would determine their own peace terms, international powers would then also be called upon to guarantee the settlement, complementing the regional guarantee structure. In this context, workshop participants discussed the question of what would move global powers, such as the United States and Russia, to take on the responsibilities of guarantors for the peace of the region. Here the parallel with the external guarantee of Westphalia by France and Sweden proved to be instructive. The foreign crowns, particularly France, were aware of the critical importance of the Holy Roman Empire in the European state system and were intent upon preventing the Empire falling under the dominance of the Habsburg Emperor or any other single potentate. France's external guarantee furthered this goal. Similarly, the Middle East today cannot be ignored by global powers; its geo-strategic salience, its oil reserves and the danger it presents as a geopolitical flashpoint ensure that. It would be in the interests of the US and Russia for the Middle East to be taken out of ongoing international rivalry, preventing conflict from spreading beyond the region, just as it was in the interests of the foreign crowns to prevent a spill-over effect from central Europe by neutralising the Empire. The Westphalian experience shows that self-interested warring parties like Russia and the United States in the Middle East can take on the mantle of effective guarantors of peace in a post-conflict era if the settlement is calibrated to be mutually beneficial. The Westphalian example also demonstrates that the guarantee can be effective even when guarantors include former enemies (France and the Emperor), just as relations between some of the proposed guarantors today are poor (US and Iran; Saudi Arabia and Iran; US and Russia). Unfortunately, the US might currently be less willing to sign up to the commitments of a guarantor than many regional powers would be. Similarly, although the EU was said to have a self-interest in a regional settlement and in avoiding spill-over, it nonetheless lacks real influence and the willingness to use force, which would be a prerequisite for a credible guarantor. Russia has established itself as a major player in Syria and the wider region and therefore is a key power in negotiating—and, more importantly, securing—peace.

The guarantee clauses were among the most controversial features of the Westphalian peace treaty because many, especially the Catholics, were wary of giving the external powers, especially France, a legal title to intervene in the German Empire. Nowadays, especially since the American-led invasion of Iraq in 2003, the idea of external intervention is highly unpopular in the Middle East. Yet the Westphalian model shows how the threat of destructive foreign interventions, such as those that occurred during the Thirty Years War, could be subjected to clearly stipulated legal mechanisms and parameters, and thereby become guarantees for peace. Westphalia thus led to a 'juridification' of intervention. One of the elements missing from the Westphalian guarantee was an adjudicating body to determine when a breach of the treaty terms had indeed taken place, and whether the guarantee could therefore be activated. In the contemporary scenario, participants of the workshops discussed the role that the UN might play in this respect. While the UN structure has a high degree of legitimacy, some felt this comes at the cost of effectiveness.

A focus on interests and crisis defusion

One of the chief lessons of the treaties of Münster and Osnabrück is that a negotiated settlement should seek to harmonise the various interests of the main actors. The focus should be on those powers that are the main drivers of conflict, either in terms of fielding armed forces or in supporting proxies. If a settlement can be reached which represents a balance between the vital interests of the main belligerents and their sponsors, then peace is possible. A corollary of this is that moral absolutes such as religious truth and ideology must be set aside as far as possible.

The primary objective in balancing interests is peace and crisis containment. A focus on interests allows for a rational cost-benefit analysis, which is necessary because conflict will continue as long as the major powers deem it to be in their interests to persist with a confrontational stance. At the congress of Westphalia, a focus on interest showed that questions of religious and theological truth needed to be bracketed out, and a compromise worked out between the interests of the great powers and those of the Imperial Estates. It is noteworthy that it was often the smallest Imperial Estates with virtually no military capabilities or actually none at all that were the most uncompromising in their attitude towards religion, as long as their lands were not under enemy occupation. Having no geo-strategic and military clout and not suffering as terribly as others from the effects of the war produced an intransigence in religious matters that other powers, which had military and geopolitical capabilities to lose and to bargain with, could not afford, despite early modern morality prescribing what would now be regarded as a religiously extremist stance.[25]

In the Middle East, such an approach which focuses primarily on a balance of interests would imply relegating moral absolutes, such as an insistence on identifying the true faith or an insistence on democratic forms of government. Instead one would need to focus on creating a balance between the interests of Saudi Arabia, Iran, Turkey, the United States, Russia and others, one which all these powers could live with. This does not imply that the region should be carved up by hegemonic powers, or that populations' aspirations should be suppressed. Indeed, the chaos, wars and terrorism resulting from justified rebellions against tyrannical rule from 2011 onwards demonstrate that, objectively, good governance and respect for citizens' basic rights are in the major states' interests, because a suppression of these rights can easily lead to domestic unrest, which has unpredictable and potentially deleterious implications for regional security.

Religious stipulations and the juridification of sectarian conflict

One of the most impressive diplomatic masterstrokes of the Westphalian peace was the way in which moral imperatives relating to religion and faith were set aside by bracketing out contentious and intractable questions of theological truth. The Westphalia treaties did this by improving the juridification of sectarian conflict, ensuring that religious conflicts were regulated legally and politically, thereby removing their propensity to cause armed conflict: this was in the interests of all the main actors represented at the congress. The religious terms had nothing to do with enlightened notions of universal religious toleration, because Westphalia predates such ideas. Instead, achieving a viable security order was the primary objective. Confessional disputes were a major obstacle to peace, as mutual mistrust prevailed after generations of sectarian strife. Thus, confessional arrangements needed to be settled in meticulous detail and placed under the umbrella of the guarantee in order to instil a measure of trust in the viability of the settlement, especially on the part of the Protestants who feared a resumption of confessional persecution and a counter-strike by the Catholics after the war.

Whether it makes sense to attempt to transfer such idiosyncratic stipulations to the Middle East is questionable. The religious terms of the treaty of Osnabrück were mainly designed to defuse the potential for conflict arising from contested ownership of churches, monasteries and other religious institutions, as well as from princely conversions. These issues are far less salient in the current Middle East. On the other hand, 're-setting' confessional conditions to a previous date, along the lines of the Westphalian normative year, might possibly be helpful in facilitating the return of religious and ethnic minorities to their previous homes in Iraq and Syria before the persecutions and massacres by the Islamic State. More controversially, such a temporal re-setting might even allow for a return of Palestinian first-generation exiles to Israel, if the major powers were to come to an agreement that this should form part of the overall settlement. Such a re-set might also constitute a good face-saving measure because it is almost banal in its simplicity and it applies uniformly to all.

More worthy of emulation, however, are the Westphalian principles of power-sharing among confessional groups and the guaranteed rights of minorities, as in the Westphalian provision that no one could be excluded from office or schools on the basis of their religion. Such provisions can form the basis of inclusive socio-political systems which foster stability and therefore peace. However, one should also be aware of the shortcomings of the Westphalian religious terms, which, far from secularising the Empire or removing confessional divisiveness, had the effect of imprinting the confessional divisions permanently onto every layer of legal regulation and every aspect of the protean Imperial constitution. It encouraged many seemingly non-religious problems and disputes to be viewed through a confessional lens, because majority voting had been abolished and because it became easier to find allies among co-religionists. This led to a confrontational and over-sensitive early modern version of identity politics that modern Western observers would recognise, albeit not one based on race, gender and so on. A comparison can be drawn here with what many feel occurred to Lebanese politics after the Ta'if accord. The Westphalian stipulation banning sectarian hate speech can be considered in this context. Although restricting freedom of speech is on principle never a good idea, practicality and the interests of peace might well outweigh principle in this case, because of the potential value of such a provision in reducing tensions and de-escalating conflicts.

Linked to this was the Westphalian stipulation of a 'perpetual oblivion and amnesty' on all sides—in other words, immunity from blame and post-war prosecution for war crimes committed. While such a provision might well help encourage warring parties to sign a peace accord, it hardly corresponds to current political and legal culture, which seeks to dispel any notion of impunity among rulers and warlords. Furthermore, the presence of a general and unlimited amnesty might well serve to enhance a willingness to resume hostilities. Some form of truth and reconciliation process could conceivably be an alternative. However, the major actors might well need to come to an agreement as part of a trade-off that the most egregious war criminals—first and foremost, ISIS and the Assad regime—would face penalties that go beyond the strictures associated with a truth and reconciliation process. This is one of the areas in which there is a major gap between seventeenth-century and twenty-first-century conditions, largely due to modern media communications, and it necessitates particularly sensitive and careful handling.

The idea of channelling confessional disputes into judicial channels, on the other hand, was considered useful by most of the workshop participants. Instead of copying the instrument of a normative year, the hoped-for settlement for the Middle East would need to include assurances of minority religious and ethnic rights, within the context of an inclusive socio-political system, tailored to local specificities of the region.

Conclusion

According to the myth of the 'Westphalian system', these treaties inaugurated the modern state system, predicated upon state sovereignty and non-intervention in domestic affairs, by granting the German princes full sovereignty, among other things. As we have argued earlier in this book, Westphalia actually increased the scope for intervention in rulers' domestic affairs and reduced the princes' freedom to rule as they wished. Firstly, the normative year greatly hollowed out the princes' authority over their subjects in confessional affairs. Secondly, the Imperial judiciary, which retained jurisdiction between and within princely territories, and to which subjects could appeal by suing their governments, was made more effective and furnished with greater legitimacy at Westphalia by the provision of Protestant representation in the two supreme courts. Thirdly, the external guarantors, France and Sweden, were given a legal right to supervise adherence to Westphalian-stipulated rights and were empowered to intervene in order to enforce these if necessary.

The prospects for formalising a similar system of conditional sovereignty and juridification of intervention and of sectarian, social and political conflict in the Middle East were the subject of lively debate at the workshops. In favour of reordering the region in this way is the argument that it was precisely this form of conditional sovereignty that ensured the protection of religious minority rights, thus encouraging stability and therefore peace. Other workshop participants argued that this was too reminiscent of the post-First World War mandate system, and that the lack of sovereignty this entailed was a major cause of strife. According to this argument, sovereignty needs to be re-established and asserted rather than limited.

The topic was also discussed in the context of the debate on the necessity of regime change in Syria. Some of the participants from the region in particular (not Iran) insisted that this was a sine qua non for any settlement. Others pointed out that a compromise settlement along Westphalian lines might imply Assad's retention of governmental powers, albeit under the imposition of strict limitations guaranteed by outside powers. Similarly, the authority of princes over the confessional rights of their subjects was severely limited at Westphalia—a limitation of governmental rule which was, crucially, placed under international guarantee and therefore potentially subject to international, collective enforcement. According to a Westphalian solution of conditional sovereignty, it is essential that guarantors police norms of behaviour not only *between* states, but also *within* states, where necessary, in pursuance of stability. This is because otherwise, as we have seen, domestic unrest tends to escalate to regional conflict. It was recognised by many that states such as Syria, Iraq and Yemen already lack meaningful sovereignty. Then and now, there was and would be a certain hypocrisy in the institution of the guarantee (at least on the part of states such as Saudi Arabia), as the external guarantor would uphold rights in other regions that were being denied under the guarantor's own domestic arrangements—as was the case with France and Sweden after Westphalia too.

* * *

The Middle East is in dire need of a post-crisis regional order. Hot wars must be resolved, and the cold ones contained. What kind of regional order could be established during a peace congress which takes advantage of the diplomatic lessons outlined above? The Holy Roman Empire provides a potentially useful model for the pacification of regions and the de-escalation of crises through the concept and practice of 'juridification'—the channelling of potentially armed conflict into peaceful tracks, primarily litigation and lawsuits, but also diplomacy and politics. In 1495 the Empire established the juridification of social and political conflict among its territorial states. In 1555 and, more successfully, in 1648, the juridification of religious conflict was established. Also in 1648, the juridification of external intervention was enshrined for the first time in international and constitutional law. Interventions in the domestic affairs of other states are ubiquitous in history, both before and after 1648. The great achievement of Westphalia was to erect a viable structure that not only defused the conflict potential of religious and other disputes within a divided and fractious polity, but also in theory juridified the tendencies of armed external intervention in that region. Related to this, the Empire was uncoupled from the ongoing great power rivalry between the House of Habsburg and France. Settling both dangers was essential because the Empire was central to the European system and its states, just as the Middle East occupies a crucial geopolitical location in the world today.

With peace and stability as its ultimate goal, formalising a similar system of juridification along with conditional sovereignty for parts of the Middle East could constitute the core of a new, Westphalian order for the Middle East, based this time on the real Westphalia, not the myth. As was the case with Westphalia for Germany, the proposed 'Westphalia for the Middle East' peace process will amount to a constitutional convention for the region, or at least for a core de-escalation region in it. The failed and fragile states of the region which are the main focus of the conflict—Syria, Iraq, Yemen and perhaps Lebanon—would be remodelled as a neutralised and pacified de-escalation zone under a two-tier system of regional and international guarantee, uncoupling the Middle East from ongoing global geopolitical conflict, very much along the lines of the peace order created for the Empire at Westphalia. The states in this core pacified zone would need to adopt the relevant terms of the peace settlement as part of their constitutions, just as the Holy Roman Empire adopted the Peace of Westphalia as a fundamental constitutional law at the Regensburg Imperial Diet of 1653–4. The signatories would guarantee their own peace: the regional guarantors would be Saudi Arabia, Iran, Turkey, Egypt and the remaining states of the region, and the international guarantors would be the United States, Russia and the EU. One must also learn from the shortcomings of Westphalia, for example by setting up an effective arbitration body to determine how and if the guarantee is to be activated, and to establish mechanisms to prevent an abuse of the guarantee, like that attempted by France after 1648. In the neutralised core security zone, the use of force between and within states would be banned and citizens given the right to appeal against their rulers to supra-statal appeal courts, modelled on the supreme judicial tribunals of the Empire, in defence of their basic human rights as well as religious and property rights, which would also be clearly defined in the peace treaty. This could provide a safety valve against popular discontent erupting into Arab Spring-style rebellions and the danger of them triggering regional conflict.

More inclusive and tolerant socio-economic systems would be imposed on the constituent states of the security zone, on the basis of power-sharing arrangements similar to those adopted at Westphalia, as the lack of such rights was a contributing factor to the 2011 rebellions. In the case of repeated breaches of treaty terms or of recognised rights by the governments of the security zone, the guarantors could then legally intervene in the states in question, after a sequence of appeals and adjudication at a higher instance still to be created. This would serve to 'detoxify' and pacify the states in question, just as Westphalia detoxified the Holy Roman Empire. The main grievances against autocratic, tyrannical rule would be removed, and therefore destructive interventions in domestic conflicts would be transformed into external guarantees of peace, with the guarantors upholding a set of norms and terms that will have been negotiated by all the main powers, and that will therefore represent a mutually tolerable balance of their respective interests. The guarantee could thus build on a functioning balance of power and buttress a system of checks and balances. In this way, all three of the main causes of instability and conflict in the Middle East identified in chapter 2—a crisis of legitimacy, the pernicious impact of great power rivalry, and sectarianism—would be addressed and calmed, if not completely resolved.

We have argued in this book that the primary value of Westphalia as an inspiration to end conflict in the Middle East lies less in its treaty content per se than in its peacemaking techniques and its diplomatic lessons—chiefly, the inclusive multilateral congress and methods of securing the longevity of the peace. But the preceding has also indicated, more tentatively, that elements from the Westphalia treaties could be of potential value as possible models for a new regional order, because they so effectively managed conflict resolution and de-escalation within a conflict-prone and divided region, while simultaneously managing its relationship to the broader international environment. This is a crucial lesson, because the Thirty Years War, like the current Middle

Eastern war, fed off a destructive cross-fertilisation between domestic ills and international geopolitical rivalry. By successfully addressing all the involved and interlocking levels of conflicts, Westphalia created a successful peace order for central Europe while conflict continued elsewhere. Such a feat is worth emulating, and, as the experience of the 1640s demonstrates, it should not be considered overambitious.

NOTES

FOREWORD

1. C.V. Wedgwood, *The Thirty Years War* (London, 1992, first ed. 1938), 526.

PREFACE by Nora Müller and Elisabeth von Hammerstein

1. Quoted in the report *Reinventing 'Westphalia': Historical Lessons for a future peace in the Middle East*, Körber-Stiftung, 2017, 4–5.
2. Quoted in ibid., 2.

PREFACE by Ralf Beste and Maike Thier

1. Margaret MacMillan, *The Uses and Abuses of History* (London, 2010), 154.

1. INTRODUCTION: THE RELEVANCE OF THE THIRTY YEARS WAR AND WESTPHALIA FOR THE MIDDLE EAST TODAY

1. Speech delivered at the 2017 Munich Security Conference, https://www.koerber-stiftung.de/en/a-westphalia-for-the-middle-east/events/19022017-reinventing-westphalia.
2. Raghida Dergham, 'The Westphalian model to resolve conflicts in the Middle East', *Huffington Post*, 7 May 2017, https://www.huffingtonpost.com/entry/the-westphalian-model-to-resolve-conflicts-in-the-middle_us_590eab19e4b046ea176aec29.
3. Leopold von Ranke, 'Preface: Histories of the Latin and Germanic nations from 1494–1514', in Fritz Stern, ed., *The Varieties of History: From Voltaire to the Present* (2nd ed., New York, 1973), 57.
4. E.g. Konrad Repgen, 'Vom Nutzen der Historie', in Amalie Fössel and Christoph Kampmann, eds., *Wozu Historie Heute? Beiträge zu einer Standortbestimmung im fachübergreifenden Gespräch* (Cologne, 1996), 167–83.
5. Richard Haass, 'The new Thirty Years War', *Project Syndicate*, 21 July 2014, https://

www.project-syndicate.org/commentary/richard-n—haass-argues-that-the-middle-east-is-less-a-problem-to-be-solved-than-a-condition-to-be-managed?barrier=accessreg; Martin van Creveld, 'A Thirty Years War?', http://www.martin-van-creveld.com/a-thirty-years-war/; Andreas Whittam Smith, 'To fight Isis we need to learn from the era of Calvinism', *The Independent*, 16 Dec. 2015, http://www.independent.co.uk/voices/to-fight-isis-we-need-to-learn-from-the-era-of-calvinism-a6775841.html.

6. Richard N. Haass, 'World Order 2.0: The case for sovereign obligation', *Foreign Affairs*, Jan./Feb. 2017, https://www.foreignaffairs.com/articles/2016–12–12/world-order-20.
7. Dorothée Goetze and Lena Oetzel, 'Der #Bonn1648-Jahresrückblick', *Rheinische Geschichte—wissenschaftlich bloggen*, 20.12.2017, http://histrhen.landesgeschichte.eu/2017/12/jahresrueckblick-bonn1648/.
8. There is body of political science literature that treats comparative peace processes. See Jonathan Tonge, *Comparative Peace Processes* (Cambridge, 2014); Cynthia J. Arnson, ed., *Comparative Peace Processes in Latin America* (Stanford, 1999).
9. Christian-P. Hanelt and Christian Koch, 'A Gulf CSC could bring peace and greater security to the Middle East', Bertelsmann Stiftung, Spotlight Europe, July 2015.
10. Conference on Security and Co-operation in Europe Final Act, Helsinki, 1975, 1(a), VII, http://www.osce.org/helsinki-final-act.
11. Matthew J. Burrows, 'History's lessons for resolving today's Middle East conflicts', *Atlantic Council*, Issue Brief, October 2016.
12. Siegrid Westphal, *Der Westfälische Frieden* (Munich, 2015), 10.
13. Jason Cowley, 'A dictator's apprenticeship. The Vienna through which Hitler wandered in his youth was a melting pot of decadent turmoil, the capital of an empire in decline—a "research laboratory for world destruction"', *New Statesman*, 26 April 1999, https://www.newstatesman.com/node/149036.
14. https://www.auswaertiges-amt.de/en/Newsroom/160920-bm-historikertag/283554.
15. https://www.coggs.polis.cam.ac.uk/laboratories-for-world-construction/westphalia-middle-east.
16. https://www.koerber-stiftung.de/en/a-westphalia-for-the-middle-east.html.
17. See the report *Reinventing 'Westphalia': Historical Lessons for a Future Peace in the Middle East*, Körber-Stiftung, 2017, 15.
18. See, for example, Dergham, 'The Westphalian model to resolve conflicts in the Middle East'.
19. https://www.coggs.polis.cam.ac.uk/news/report-on-workshop-elements-of-a-regional-peace-settlement-for-the-middle-east-amman-jordan-22–23-january-2017.
20. http://www.wirtschaftliche-gesellschaft.de/int-preis-des-westfaelischen-friedens/preistraeger/.

21. https://www.auswaertiges-amt.de/en/Newsroom/160712-westfaelischer-frieden/282280; https://www.auswaertiges-amt.de/en/Newsroom/160920-bm-historikertag/283554.
22. https://www.bundeskanzlerin.de/Content/DE/Rede/2017/09/2017–09–10-rede-bk-sant-egidio.html.
23. https://www.bundestag.de/presse/pressemitteilungen/2017/pm-171024-rede-schaeuble/530102.
24. E.g. Rainer Hermann, 'Die Suche nach einem Frieden. Was wir vom Westfälischen Frieden für die arabische Welt heute lernen können', *Frankfurter Allgemeine Zeitung*, 18 Aug. 2016. His thoughts are further elaborated in *Arabisches Beben. Die wahren Gründe der Krise im Nahen Osten* (Stuttgart, 2018), 196–204. See also Joost Hiltermann, 'Tackling the MENA region's intersecting conflicts', International Crisis Group report, February 2018, https://www.crisisgroup.org/middle-east-north-africa/eastern-mediterranean/syria/tackling-mena-regions-intersecting-conflicts.
25. Younes Hassar, 'The Middle East needs a Westphalian moment not new borders', *International Policy Digest*, 7 June 2016, https://intpolicydigest.org/2016/06/07/the-middle-east-needs-a-westphalian-moment-not-new-borders/.
26. E.g. Tobias von Gienanth, 'Realismus und Bescheidenheit. Ein Vergleich mit dem Dreißigjährigen Krieg ist auch heute noch lehrreich', *Internationale Politik*, July/August 2015, 84–90.
27. Herfried Münkler, *Der Dreissigjährige Krieg. Europäische Katastrophe, deutsches Trauma, 1618–1648* (Berlin, 2017), 22–31, 36–9, 817–43.
28. E.g. 'Die Geschichte der Deutschen. Von den Germanen bis zur Wiedervereinigung', *Stern Extra*, 3 (2010), 81–2.
29. See, for example, the May 2017 speech by the German foreign minister Sigmar Gabriel: https://www.auswaertiges-amt.de/de/newsroom/170522-bm-friedens-verantwortung-religionen/290118.
30. E.g. Derek Beales, *Joseph II* (2 vols., Cambridge, 1987–2009), vol. 2, 410–11; Wolfgang E.J. Weber, 'Von der normativen Herrschaftspflicht zum interessenpolitischen Instrument. Zum Konzept der Protektion in der politischen Theorie der Frühen Neuzeit', in Tilman Haug et al., *Protegierte und Protektoren* (Vienna, Cologne, Weimar, 2016), 31–48, at 44–5; Michael Hughes, *Law and Politics in Eighteenth-Century Germany: The Imperial Aulic Council in the Reign of Charles VI* (Woodbridge, 1988), 16–17; James J. Sheehan, *German History 1770–1866* (Oxford, 1994), 16.
31. E.g. Daniel Philpott, *Revolutions in Sovereignty: How Ideas Shaped Modern International Relations* (Princeton, 2001), 4, 30, 85; Michael Ross Fowler and Julie Marie Bunck, *Law, Power, and the Sovereign State: The Evolution and Application of the Concept of Sovereignty* (University Park, PA, 1995), 65; Evan Luard, *The Balance of Power: The System of International Relations, 1648–1815* (Basingstoke,

1992); Wilfried Hinsch and Dieter Janssen, *Menschenrechte militärisch schützen. Ein Plädoyer für Humanitäre Intervention* (Bonn, 2006), 58, 88; Justin Rosenberg, *The Empire of Civil Society: A Critique of the Realist Theory of International Relations* (London and New York, 1994), 138.

32. T.J. Lawrence, *Essays on Some Disputed Questions in Modern International Law* (Cambridge, 1885), 206; Lassa Oppenheim, *International Law*, vol. 1 (London, 1905), 60; Andrea Rapisardi Mirabelli, *Le Congres de Westphalie* (Leyden, 1929), 14–15.
33. Robert Gilpin, *War and Change in World Politics* (Cambridge, 1981), 29f, 36f; Gert Krell, *Weltbilder und Weltordnung. Einführung in die Theorie der internationalen Beziehungen* (3rd ed., Baden-Baden, 2004), 113; Lynn H. Miller, *Global Order: Values and Power in International Politics* (Boulder and London, 1995).
34. Derek Croxton, *Westphalia: The Last Christian Peace* (New York, 2013), 351–62; Peter H. Wilson, *Europe's Tragedy: A New History of the Thirty Years War* (London, 2010), 776–8; Georg Schmidt, 'Der Westfälische Frieden—eine neue Ordnung für das alte Reich?,' in Reinhard Mußgnug, ed., *Wendemarken in der Deutschen Verfassungsgeschichte: Tagung der Vereinigung für Verfassungsgeschichte* (Berlin, 1993), 45–84.
35. Andreas Osiander, 'Sovereignty, international relations, and the Westphalian myth', *International Organization*, 55, no. 2 (2001), 251–87.
36. Stephane Beaulac, 'The Westphalian legal orthodoxy—myth or reality?', *Journal of the History of International Law*, 2 (2000), 148–77.
37. Derek Croxton, 'The Peace of Westphalia of 1648 and the origins of sovereignty', *International History Review*, 21, no. 3 (1999), 569–91; Heinz Duchhardt, '"Westphalian System". Zur Problematik einer Denkfigur', *Historische Zeitschrift*, 269 (1999), 305–15.
38. Anthony McGraw, 'Globalization and global politics', in J. Baylis, S. Smith et al., eds., *The Globalization of World Politics* (Oxford, 2011), 23; Robert Jackson, *The Global Covenant: Human Conduct in a World of States* (Oxford, 2000), 385, 398.
39. Arnaud Blin, *1648, La Paix de Westphalie, ou la naissance de l'Europe politique moderne* (Brussels, 2006); Herfried Münkler, *Der Wandel des Krieges. Von der Symmetrie zur Asymmetrie* (Weilerswist, 2006), 32–5.
40. Albrecht Randelzhofer, *Völkerrechtliche Aspekte des Heiligen Römischen Reiches nach 1648* (Berlin, 1967); O. Kimminich, *Deutsche Verfassungsgeschichte* (Baden-Baden, 1987), 215–28; Heinrich Mitteis, *Deutsche Rechtsgeschichte* (Munich, 1969), 217; H. Boldt, *Deutsche Verfassungsgeschichte* (2nd ed., Munich, 1990), vol. 1, 276.
41. Gene M. Lyons and Michael Mastanduno, eds., *Beyond Westphalia? State Sovereignty and International Intervention* (Baltimore, 1995); Mark W. Zacher, 'The decaying pillars of the Westphalian temple: implications for international order and governance', in James N. Rosenau, ed., *Governance without Government: Order and Change in World Politics* (New York, 1992), 58–101.

42. Sasson Sofer, 'The prominence of historical demarcations: Westphalia and the new world order', *Diplomacy and Statecraft*, 20, no. 1 (2009), 1–19.
43. Stephen D. Krasner, *Sovereignty: Organized Hypocrisy* (Princeton, 1999).
44. Gerhard Göhler, 'Politische Theorien des 17. und 18. Jahrhundert in Deutschland: ein Überblick', in Gerhard Göhler and Bernd Heidenreich, eds., *Politische Theorien des 17. und 18. Jhrs. Staat und Politik in Deutschland* (Darmstadt/Mainz, 2011), 10–36, at 11–12; Magnus Rüde, *England und Kurpfalz im werdenden Mächteeuropa (1608–1632). Konfession—Dynastie—kulturelle Ausdrucksformen* (Stuttgart, 2007), 15, 300.
45. John G. Gagliardo, *Reich and Nation: The Holy Roman Empire as Idea and Reality, 1763–1806* (Bloomington and London, 1980), viii, 18, 25, 45; Andreas Dorpalen, *German History in Marxist Perspective: The East German Approach* (London, 1985), 136.
46. Johannes Burkhardt, 'Der Westfälische Friede und die Legende von der landesherrlichen Souveränität', in Jörg Engelbrecht and Stephan Laux, eds., *Landes- und Reichsgeschichte: Festschrift für Hansgeorg Molitor zum 65. Geburtstag* (Bielefeld, 2004), 199–220.
47. For the refutation, see Westphal, *Der Westfälische Frieden*, 105; Croxton, *Last Christian Peace*, 354–56.
48. Leo Gross, 'The Peace of Westphalia 1648–1948', *American Journal of International Law*, 42 (1948), 20–41, esp. 20, 28.
49. Croxton, *Last Christian Peace*, 352.
50. Heinz Duchhardt, 'Das "Westfälische System": Realität und Mythos', in Hillard von Thiessen and Christian Windler, eds., *Akteure der Außenbeziehungen. Netzwerke Und Interkulturalität Im Historischen Wandel* (Cologne, 2010), 393–402.
51. Gottfried Wilhelm Leibniz, *Sämtliche Schriften und Briefe* (Berlin, 1983), series IV, vol. 2, 21; Emer de Vattel, *The Law of Nations, or, Principles of the Law of Nature*, ed. Béa Kapossy and Richard Whatmore (Indianapolis, 2008), 683–4; Gottfried Achenwall, *Geschichte der allgemeineren Europäischen Staatshändel des vorigen und ietzigen Jahrhunderts im Grundriss der europäischen Geschichte* (Göttingen, 1761), 84. Another aspect of the Westphalian myth that was already argued by some natural law writers is the notion that the treaties of 1648 granted Switzerland and the Dutch Republic full independence from the Holy Roman Empire: e.g. Vattel, *The Law of Nations*, 212, 696.
52. Michael Stolleis, *Geschichte des öffentlichen Rechts in Deutschland. Band I, 1600–1800* (Munich, 1988), 233, 276–7; Knud Haakonssen, 'German natural law', in Mark Goldie and Robert Wokler, eds., *The Cambridge History of Eighteenth-Century Political Thought* (Cambridge, 2006), 251–90, at 256–7; Notker Hammerstein, 'Christian Thomasius', in Bernd Heidenreich and Gerhard Göhler, eds., *Politische Theorien des 17. und 18. Jahrhunderts: Staat und Politik in*

Deutschland (Darmstadt, 2011), 123–4, 13; Detlef Döring, 'Der Westfälische Frieden in der Sicht Samuel von Pufendorfs', *Zeitschrift für Historische Forschung*, 16, no. 3 (1999), 349–64, at 353.

53. Johann Gustav Droysen, *Geschichte der preußischen Politik, Teil 3, Abteilung 1* (Berlin, 1861), 338f. ('The Reich actually ceased to exist, there only remained sovereign territories.') Other examples: Friedrich Rühs, *Historische Entwickelung des Einflusses Frankreichs und der Franzosen auf Deutschland und die Deutschen* (Berlin, 1815), 61, 75; Georg Winter, 'Der Dreißigjährige Krieg', in Ferdinand Hirsch, ed., *Gebhardts Handbuch der Deutschen Geschichte* (3rd ed., Stuttgart, 1906), vol. 2, 182.
54. E.g. Johannes Burckhardt, 'Das größte Friedenswerk der Neuzeit', *Geschichte in Wissenschaft und Unterricht*, vol. 49 (1998), 592–612.
55. Selim Can Sazak, 'No Westphalia for the Middle East', *Foreign Affairs*, 27 October 2016, https://www.foreignaffairs.com/articles/middle-east/2016-10-27/no-westphalia-middle-east.
56. http://peaceofwestphalia.org/?p=308.
57. Sazak, 'No Westphalia for the Middle East'.
58. The best English-language general works on the Empire are Peter H. Wilson, *The Holy Roman Empire: A Thousand Years of Europe's History* (London, 2016), and Joachim Whaley, *Germany and the Holy Roman Empire* (2 vols., Oxford, 2012), though Veronica Wedgwood's classic account is still worth reading.
59. Patrick Milton, 'Intervening against tyrannical rule in the Holy Roman Empire during the seventeenth and eighteenth centuries', *German History*, 33, no. 1 (2015), 1–29.
60. Helmut Neuhaus, '"Defension"—Das frühneuzeitliche Heilige Römische Reich als Verteidigungsgemeinschaft', in Stephan Wendehorst and Siegrid Westphal, eds., *Lesebuch Altes Reich* (Munich, 2006), 119–26.
61. Wolfgang Burgdorf, *Reichskonstitution und Nation. Verfassungsreformprojekte für das Heilige Römische Reich deutscher Nation im politischen Schrifttum von 1648 bis 1806* (Mainz, 1998).

2. CHALLENGES AND CRISES IN THE MIDDLE EAST

1. Quoted in the report *Reinventing 'Westphalia': Historical Lessons for a future peace in the Middle East*, Körber-Stiftung, 2017, 4–5.
2. Ibid., 2.
3. In addition to the material cited below, the following draws on the unpublished papers presented by Toby Matthiesen, Ali Ansari, Payam Ghalehdar, Gareth Stansfield, and Raphaël Lefèvre at the first seminar of 'A Westphalia for the Middle East', London, 2 March 2016.
4. Herfried Münkler has also argued that for lessons to be drawn for the Middle East from the Thirty Years War, both sets of conflicts need to be treated as interlocking,

rather than piecemeal: 'Was der Dreißigjährige Krieg mit heutigen Kriegen zu tun hat', *Siegel Online* interview by Jan Fleischhauer and Cordula Meyer with Herfried Münkler, http://www.spiegel.de/spiegel/herfried-muenkler-ueber-den-dreissig-jaehrigen-krieg-a-1175447.html; 'Mit Maria kämpft's sich leichter', *Die Zeit* interview by Raol Löbbert and Fabian Klask with Herfried Münkler, http://www.zeit.de/2017/47/herfried-muenkler-dreissigjaehriger-krieg-reformationsjahr/komplettansicht. For another example of the argument that the Middle East crisis needs to be approached as a regional whole, see Galip Dalay, 'Break-up of the Middle East: Will we see a new regional order?', *Middle East Eye*, 22 Aug. 2017, http://www.middleeasteye.net/essays/middle-east-fragmentation-opportunity-regional-co-operation-1111336507.

5. James Barr, *A Line in the Sand: Britain, France and the Struggle That Shaped the Middle East* (London, 2011).
6. Lisa Anderson, 'Absolutism and the resilience of monarchy in the Middle East', *Political Science Quarterly*, 106, no. 1 (1991), 1–15.
7. See forthcoming dissertation research by Galip Dalay (Istanbul).
8. Anton La Guardia, 'Middle East special report: The clash within', *The Economist*, 14 May 2016.
9. Peter H. Wilson, 'The Thirty Years War as the Empire's constitutional crisis', in in R.J.W. Evans, Michael Schaich and Peter H. Wilson, eds., *The Holy Roman Empire 1495–1806* (Oxford, 2011), 95–114.
10. David Hirst, *Beware of Small States: Lebanon, Battleground of the Middle East* (New York, 2010).
11. Marc Lynch, *The New Arab Wars: Uprisings and Anarchy in the Middle East* (New York, 2016), 28.
12. Jonathan Marcus, 'Why Saudi Arabia and Iran are bitter rivals', *BBC News*, 18 Nov. 2017, http://www.bbc.co.uk/news/world-middle-east-42008809.
13. Lynch, *New Arab Wars*, 24–5, 34.
14. Quoted in https://www.reuters.com/article/us-mideast-crisis-syria-iran/irans-velayati-says-east-syria-idlib-to-be-cleared-soon-idUSKBN1D82D3.
15. 'Iran and Saudi Arabia: Friends and foes in the region', *BBC News*, 10 Nov. 2017, http://www.bbc.co.uk/news/world-middle-east-41945860; Jonathan Marcus, 'Russia in Syria: "Victory" in war but can Moscow win the peace?', *BBC News*, 27 Nov. 2017, http://www.bbc.co.uk/news/world-middle-east-42082615.
16. Holly Ellyatt, 'Could Saudi Arabia and Iran really go to war?', https://www.cnbc.com/2017/11/22/could-saudi-arabia-and-iran-really-go-to-war.html.
17. Michael Axworthy, 'Regime change in Iran would be a disaster for everyone', *Foreign Policy*, 18 July 2017, https://foreignpolicy.com/2017/07/18/regime-change-in-iran-would-be-a-disaster-for-everyone-trump-tillerson/.
18. 'America's neglect and confusion aggravate problems in the Arab world: Giving free rein to Saudi Arabia is destabilising the region', *The Economist*, 2 Dec. 2017.

19. Jonathan Marcus, 'Israel and Saudi Arabia: What's shaping the covert "alliance"?', *BBC News*, 24 Nov. 2017, http://www.bbc.co.uk/news/world-middle-east-42094105.
20. 'The big purge in Saudi Arabia: Muhammad bin Salman has swept aside those who challenge his power', *The Economist*, 9 Nov. 2017.
21. 'The Middle East's punchbag: Iran and Saudi Arabia take their rivalry to Lebanon', *The Economist*, 16 Nov. 2017.
22. 'The Saudi hand in Saad Hariri's resignation as Lebanese prime minister', *The Economist*, 11 Nov. 2017.
23. Kristian Coates Ulrichsen, 'Implications of the Qatar crisis for regional security in the Gulf', *Al Sharq Forum Expert Brief*, June 2017.
24. 'Why the Gulf Co-operation Council can't co-operate', *The Economist*, 7 Dec. 2017.
25. Lynch, *New Arab Wars*, 82.
26. Georg Schmidt, *Der Dreissigjährige Krieg* (Munich, 2010), 50–1.
27. As argued by Galip Dalay, 'A difference of opinion? Fissures in US-Turkish relations after Syria', *Brookings Institution*, 26 Jan. 2018.
28. Selin Girit, 'Why is Turkey standing up for Qatar?', *BBC News*, 14 June 2017, http://www.bbc.co.uk/news/world-middle-east-40262713.
29. Cengiz Candar, 'Turkey's misguided Middle East policy: From Syria, Iraq to the Gulf', *Al-Monitor*, 13 Nov. 2017, https://www.al-monitor.com/pulse/originals/2017/11/turkey-misguided-policy-displays-itself-in-three-main-areas.html.
30. Anton Mardasov, 'Latest Syria peace talks solidify final de-escalation zone', *Al-Monitor*, 22 Sept. 2017, http://www.al-monitor.com/pulse/originals/2017/09/syria-peace-astana-zones-opposition-kurds-assad-russia.html#ixzz5402RbEHG.
31. Anne Barnard, 'Syrian peace talks in Russia: 1,500 delegates, mostly pro-Assad', *New York Times*, 30 Jan. 2018, https://www.nytimes.com/2018/01/30/world/middleeast/syria-russia-sochi-talks.html.
32. Sinan Hatahet, 'The prospects of a political transition in Syria', *Al Sharq Forum Expert Brief*, December 2017.
33. Daniel Gerlach, *Herrschaft über Syrien. Macht und Manipulation unter Assad* (Hamburg, 2015).
34. Anton La Guardia, 'Special report: The clash within', *The Economist*, 14 May 2016.
35. Ian Black, 'Fear of a Shia full moon', *The Guardian*, 26 Jan. 2007.
36. Roland Czada, 'Ein "Westfälischer Friede" für die Krisenherde der Gegenwart?', *Osnabrücker Jahrbuch: Frieden und Wissenschaft*, 24 (2017), 159–79, at 174.
37. Michael Axworthy, 'Sunni vs. Shia: The roots of Islam's civil war', *New Statesman*, 29 Aug. 2017, https://www.newstatesman.com/world/middle-east/2017/08/sunni-vs-shia-roots-islam-s-civil-war.
38. Lynch, *New Arab Wars*, 15; Frederic Wehry, *Sectarian Politics in the Gulf* (New York, 2014).

39. Toby Matthiesen, *The Other Saudis: Shiism, Dissent and Sectarianism* (Cambridge, 2014).
40. Toby Matthiesen, *Sectarian Gulf: Bahrain, Saudi Arabia, and the Arab Spring That Wasn't* (Stanford, 2013).
41. Laurent Louer, *Transnational Shia Politics: Religious and Political Networks in the Gulf* (Oxford, 2012).
42. Bruce Riedel, 'Influence-rich Saudis blow through Sunni unity', *Al-Monitor*, 15 June 2017, https://www.al-monitor.com/pulse/originals/2017/06/saudi-arabia-unity-sunni-states-trump-iran-salman.html.
43. Toby Matthiesen, 'The sectarian Gulf vs. the Arab Spring', *Foreign Policy*, 8 Oct. 2013, http://foreignpolicy.com/2013/10/08/the-sectarian-gulf-vs-the-arab-spring/.
44. Axworthy, 'Sunni vs Shia'; for the continued importance of religion after 1648, see David Onnekink, ed., *War and Religion after Westphalia, 1648–1713* (Farnham and Burlington, VT, 2010), and Jürgen Luh, *Unheiliges Römisches Reich. Der konfessionelle Gegensatz, 1648 bis 1806* (Potsdam, 1995).

3. FROM RELIGIOUS PEACE TO THE THIRTY YEARS WAR: MULTIPLE CRISES IN EUROPE AND THE HOLY ROMAN EMPIRE, 1555–1648

1. Quoted in Tryntje Helfferich, ed., *The Thirty Years War: A Documentary History* (Indianapolis, 2009), 21–9.
2. Quoted in ibid., 102.
3. There is a historiographical debate about origins of the war. Some mainly anglophone historians such as Geoffrey Parker, ed., *The Thirty Years War* (New York, 1993) view the Thirty Years War as subsumed in a broader international problem, the so-called general crisis of the seventeenth century, whereas others, such as Peter H. Wilson, *Europe's Tragedy: A New History of the Thirty Years War* (London, 2009) and Georg Schmidt, *Der Dreissigjährige Krieg* (Munich, 2010), view it as a distinctly German (i.e. Imperial) war, and emphasise the Habsburgs' problems in managing their hereditary lands of Austria and Bohemia as territorial rulers, with these dynastic problems affecting their ability to manage the Holy Roman Empire as a whole as Emperors. Historians such as Christoph Kampmann, *Europa und das Reich im Dreißigjährigen Krieg* (Stuttgart, 2013) steer a middle course between these two interpretations with an emphasis on local and Imperial problems which then irreversibly and incrementally escalated to the international level.
4. The following draws on Christoph Kampmann, 'International context and internationalisation of the Thirty Years War', unpublished paper presented at seminar two of 'A Westphalia for the Middle East', Cambridge, 19 March 2016.
5. Heinz Schilling, *Konfessionalisierung und Staatsinteressen. Internationale Beziehungen 1559–1660* (Paderborn, 2007), 385–92.

6. John H. Elliott, 'A Europe of composite monarchies', *Past and Present*, 137 (1992), 48–71.
7. Schilling, *Konfessionalisierung*, 393.
8. Brendan Simms, 'Europe's shifting balance of power', in Hamish Scott, ed., *The Oxford Handbook of Early Modern European History, 1350–1750, vol. 2: Culture and Power* (Oxford, 2015), 649–50.
9. Brendan Simms, *Europe: The Struggle for Supremacy, 1453 to the Present* (London, 2013), chs. 1–2.
10. Kampmann, *Europa und das Reich*, 10–11; Schilling, *Konfessionalisierung*, 462–77; Wilson, *Europe's Tragedy*, 116–29.
11. Geoffrey Parker, *The Army of Flanders and the Spanish Road 1567–1659* (Cambridge, 1972).
12. Kampmann, *Europa und das Reich*, 7–10; Schilling, *Konfessionalisierung*, 436–48; Wilson, *Europe's Tragedy*, 129–61.
13. Kampmann, *Europa und das Reich*, 11–15; Schilling, *Konfessionalisierung*, 308–45, 448–57,498–506; Wilson, *Europe's Tragedy*, 168–96.
14. Kampmann, *Europa und das Reich*, 15–16; Schilling, *Konfessionalisierung*, 457–61; Wilson, *Europe's Tragedy*, 76–106.
15. In addition to the material cited below, the following draws on Michael Kaiser, 'Loss of certainties, fear and distrust: The multiple crisis which led the way to war', unpublished paper presented at seminar 2 of 'A Westphalia for the Middle East', Cambridge, 19 March 2016, and Kampmann, *Europa und das Reich*, 17–27.
16. Wilson, *Holy Roman Empire*, 19–33.
17. Luise Schorn-Schütte, *Die Reformation. Vorgeschichte, Verlauf, Wirkung* (Munich, 2011).
18. Axel Gotthard, *Der Augsburger Religionsfrieden* (Münster, 2004).
19. Quoted in Patrick Milton, 'The early eighteenth-century German confessional crisis: The juridification of religious conflict in the re-confessionalised politics of the Holy Roman Empire', *Central European History*, 49, no. 1 (2016), 39–68, at 44.
20. Wilson, *Europe's Tragedy*, 197–238.
21. Kampmann, *Europa und das Reich*, 17; Wilson, *Europe's Tragedy*, 239–66.
22. Robert Bireley, *The Refashioning of Catholicism, 1450–1700: A Reassessment of the Counter-Reformation* (Basingstoke, 1999).
23. Kampmann, *Europa und das Reich*, 26.
24. Alison D. Anderson, *On the Verge of War: International Relations and the Jülich-Kleve Succession Dispute (1609–1614)* (Boston, 1999).
25. Kaiser, 'Loss of certainties, fear and distrust'.
26. Peter H. Wilson, 'The causes of the Thirty Years War 1618–48', *English Historical Review*, 123, no. 502 (2008), 554–86.
27. Wilson, *Europe's Tragedy*, 106–16.

28. Kampmann, *Europa und das Reich*, 27–34.
29. Robert Bireley, *Religion and Politics in the Age of the Counterreformation: Emperor Ferdinand II, William Lamormaini S.J. and the Formation of Imperial Policy* (Chapel Hill, 1981); Schilling, *Konfessionalisierung*; Mark Konnert, *Early Modern Europe: The Age of Religious War, 1559–1715* (Ontario, 2006), 12.
30. Peter H. Wilson, 'Dynasty, constitution, and confession: The role of religion in the Thirty Years War', *International History Review*, 30, no. 3 (2008), 473–514.
31. Ibid.
32. Peter Wilson, 'The character of the Thirty Years War', unpublished paper presented at seminar 2 of 'A Westphalia for the Middle East', Cambridge, 19 March 2016.
33. Michael Howard, *War in European History* (Oxford, 1976), 37; C.V. Wedgwood, *The Thirty Years War* (London, 1957), 383.
34. Peter Wilson, 'Crisis containment and peace-making in the Thirty Years War' unpublished paper presented at seminar 3 of 'A Westphalia for the Middle East', Cambridge, 23 April 2016.
35. Ronald G. Asch, '"Wo der soldat hinkömbt, da ist alles sein": Military violence and atrocities in the Thirty Years War re-examined', *German History*, 18, no. 3 (2000), 291–309; David Lederer, 'The myth of the all-destructive war: Afterthoughts on German suffering, 1618–1648', *German History*, 29 (2011), 380–403.
36. S.H. Steinberg, *The Thirty Years' War and the Conflict for European Hegemony 1600–1660* (New York, 1966).
37. Repgen, 'Seit wann gibt es den Begriff "Dreißigjähriger Krieg"?', in Heinz Dollinger et al., eds., *Weltpolitik, Europagedanke, Regionalismus* (Munich, 1982), 59–70.
38. Kampmann, *Europa und das Reich*, 103–27.
39. Münkler, *Der Dreissigjährige Krieg*, 825–7.
40. Wilson, 'The character of the Thirty Years War'.
41. Johannes Burkhardt, 'Der Dreißigjährige Krieg als frühmoderner Staatsbildungskrieg', *Geschichte in Wissenschaft und Unterricht*, 45 (1994), 487–99.
42. Brynjar Lia, 'Understanding Jihadi proto-states', *Perspectives on Terrorism*, 9, no. 4 (2015), 31–41; Cole Bunzel, 'From paper state to caliphate: The ideology of the Islamic State', *The Brookings Project on U.S. Relations with the Islamic World*, Analysis Paper, no. 19, March 2015; Connor Kopchick, 'Jihadi state-building: A comparative study of Jihadis' capacity for governance', 7 Dec. 2015, http://www.e-ir.info/2015/12/07/jihadi-state-building-a-comparative-study-of-jihadis-capacity-for-governance/.
43. Wilson, *Europe's Tragedy*, 269–314.
44. Peter J. Brightwell, 'Spain and Bohemia: The decision to intervene', *European Studies Review*, 12 (1982), 117–41.
45. Kampmann, *Europa und das Reich*, 41–9.

46. Christoph Kampmann, *Reichsrebellion und kaiserliche Acht. Politische Strafjustiz im Dreißigjährigen Krieg und das Verfahren gegen Wallenstein 1634* (Münster, 1992), 47–69.
47. Kampmann, *Europa und das Reich*, 47–9.
48. Paul Douglas Lockhart, 'Denmark and the Empire: A reassessment of Danish foreign policy under King Christian IV', *Scandinavian Studies*, 64, no. 3 (1992), 390–416.
49. Paul Douglas Lockhart, *Denmark in the Thirty Years War, 1618–1648: King Christian IV and the Decline of the Oldenburg State* (Cranbury, NJ, 1996).
50. Thomas Brockmann, *Dynastie, Kaiseramt und Konfession. Politik und Ordnungsvorstellungen Ferdinands II im Dreißigjährigen Krieg* (Paderborn, 2011).
51. Pärtel Piirimäe, 'Just war in theory and practice: The legitimation of Swedish intervention in the Thirty Years War', *Historical Journal*, 45, no. 3 (2002), 499–523.
52. Wilson, *Europe's Tragedy*, 459–511.
53. Ibid., 512–53.
54. Ronald G. Asch, *The Thirty Years War: The Holy Roman Empire and Europe 1618–1648* (Basingstoke, 1997), 111.
55. Ralf-Peter Fuchs, *Ein Medium zum Frieden. Die Normaljahrsregel und die Beendigung des Dreißigjährigen Krieges* (Munich, 2010), 127–49.
56. Wilson, *Europe's Tragedy*, 565–73.
57. Randall Lesaffer, 'Defensive warfare, prevention and hegemony: The justifications for the Franco-Spanish War of 1635', *Journal of the History of International Law*, 8 (2006) 91–123, 141–79.
58. Schmidt, *Der Dreissigjährige Krieg*, 63.
59. Kampmann, *Europa und das Reich*, 116–27.
60. Quoted in Helfferich, *The Thirty Years War: A Documentary History*, 151.
61. Wilson, *Europe's Tragedy*, 588–621.
62. Ibid., 622–708; Kampmann, *Europa und das Reich*, 128–51.

4. THE PEACE CONGRESS OF MÜNSTER AND OSNABRÜCK (1643–1648) AND THE WESTPHALIAN ORDER (1648–1806)

1. Quoted in the report *Reinventing 'Westphalia': Historical Lessons for a future peace in the Middle East*, Körber-Stiftung, 2017, 13.
2. Peter Wilson, 'Crisis containment and peace-making in the Thirty Years War', unpublished paper presented at seminar 3 of 'A Westphalia for the Middle East', Cambridge, 23 April 2016.
3. Ibid.
4. Westphal, *Der Westfälische Frieden*, 13.
5. Johannes Burkhardt, 'Die Friedlosigkeit der Frühen Neuzeit. Grundlegung einer Theorie der Bellizität Europas', *Zeitschrift für Historische Forschung*, 24, no. 4 (1997), 509–74.

6. Westphal, *Der Westfälische Frieden*, 12–13; Kampmann, *Europa und das Reich*, 181–2.
7. Kampmann, *Europa und das Reich*, 183.
8. Alistair Malcolm, 'Spanish views on the Westphalia process: Congress diplomacy as eternalisation of war', unpublished paper presented at the conference 'Warum Friedenschließen so schwer ist. Der Wesfälische Friedenskongress in interdisziplinärer Perspektive', Bonn, 31 August and 1 Sept. 2017.
9. As argued by Christoph Kampmann in an unpublished paper presented at a workshop at the German Foreign Office in 2016.
10. Franz Bosbach, *Die Kosten des Westfälischen Friedenskongresses. Eine strukturgeschichtliche Untersuchung* (Münster, 1984), 224; Westphal, *Der Westfälische Frieden*, 44.
11. Fritz Dickmann, *Der Westfälische Frieden* (Münster, 1998), 189–92.
12. Ibid., 213.
13. Croxton, *Last Christian Peace*, 246.
14. Quoted in Schmidt, *Der Dressigjährige Krieg*, 73.
15. Karsten Ruppert, *Die kaiserliche Politik auf dem Westfälischen Friedenskongreß (1643–1648)* (Münster: Aschendorff, 1979).
16. Konrad Repgen, 'Die Hauptprobleme der WestfälischenFriedensverhandlungen von 1648 und ihre Lösungen', *Zeitschrift für bayerische Landesgeschichte*, 62 (1999), 399–438.
17. Niels F. May, *Zwischen fürstlicher Repräsentation undadliger Statuspolitik. Das Kongresszeremoniell bei den westfälischen Friedensverhandlungen* (Ostfildern, 2016).
18. See André Krischer, 'Souveränität als sozialer Status. Zur Funktion des diplomatischen Zeremoniells in der Frühen Neuzeit', in Ralph Kauz, Giorgio Rota and Jan-Paul Niederkorn, eds., *Diplomatisches Zeremoniell in Europa und im Mittleren Osten in der Frühen Neuzeit* (Vienna, 2009), 1–32.
19. Westphal, *Der Westfälische Frieden*, 53
20. Croxton, *Last Christian Peace*, 3.
21. Konrad Repgen, 'Maximilian Graf Trauttmansdorff—Chefunterhändler des Kaisers beim Prager und beim Westfälischen Frieden', in Guido Braun and Arno Strohmeyer, eds., *Frieden und Friedenssicherung in der Frühen Neuzeit. Das Heilige Römische Reich und Europa. Festschrift für Maximilian Lanzinner zum 65. Geburtstag* (Münster, 2013), 211–28.
22. Christoph Kampmann, 'Peace impossible? The Holy Roman Empire and the European state system in the seventeenth century', in Olaf Asbach and Peter Schröder, eds., *War, State and International Law in Seventeenth Century Europe* (Farnham, 2009), 197–210.
23. Derek Croxton, *Peacemaking in Early Modern Europe: Cardinal Mazarin and the Congress of Westphalia, 1643–1648* (Selinsgrove, 1999).

24. Repgen, 'Hauptprobleme'.
25. Croxton, *Last Christian Peace*, 246–49.
26. Dickmann, *Der Westfälische Frieden*, 212–15.
27. 'Iran and Saudi Arabia: Friends and foes in the region', *BBC News*, 10 November 2017, http://www.bbc.co.uk/news/world-middle-east-41945860.
28. Westphal, *Der Westfälische Frieden*, 53.
29. Papers by Lena Oetzel, Magnus U. Ferber and Maria-Elisabeth Brunert at Bonn conference.
30. Anuschka Tischer, 'Vom Kriegsgrund hin zum Friedensschluß: der Einfluß unterschiedlicher Faktoren auf die Formulierung von Friedensverträgen am Beispiel des Westfälischen Friedens', in Heinz Duchhardt and Martin Peters, eds., *Kalkül—Transfer—Symbol. Europäische Friedensverträge der Vormoderne* (Mainz, 2 Nov. 2006), www.ieg-mainz.de/vieg-online-beihefte/01–2006.html.
31. Anuschka Tischer, 'The international context of the conclusion of the peace', unpublished paper presented at seminar 3 of 'A Westphalia for the Middle East', 23 April 2016. See also Dickmann, *Der Westfälische Frieden*, 216–324.
32. Dickmann, *Der Westfälische Frieden*, 373–80.
33. Guido Braun, 'The political compromise between the princes' and the Emperor's prerogatives in 1648', unpublished paper presented at seminar 3 of 'A Westphalia for the Middle East', 23 April 2016. See also Dickmann, *Der Westfälische Frieden*, 325–32.
34. For this, see Dickmann, *Der Westfälische Frieden*, 343–73, 456–65. The following is based on Repgen, 'Hauptprobleme'.
35. Croxton, *Last Christian Peace*, 287–8.
36. Ralf-Peter Fuchs, 'A date for a reset: The confessional settlement of the Peace of Westphalia', unpublished paper presented at seminar 3 of 'A Westphalia for the Middle East', Cambridge, 23 April 2016. See also Ralf-Peter Fuchs, *Ein Medium zum Frieden. Die Normaljahrsregel und die Beendigung des Dreißigjährigen Krieges* (Munich, 2010), 159–212.
37. Ruppert, *Kaiserliche Politik*, 296.
38. Westphal, *Der Westfälische Frieden*, 88–90; Dickmann, *Der Westfälische Frieden*, 443–56.
39. APW II A, vol. 10 (Münster, 2015), no. 43, 182–203.
40. Ruppert, *Kaiserliche Politik*, 343f; Dickmann, *Der Westfälische Frieden*, 477–88.
41. From the Imperial perspective: Ruppert, *Kaiserliche Politik*; from the French perspective: Tischer, *Französische Diplomatie und Diplomaten*, and Croxton, *Mazarin and the Congress of Westphalia*; from the Spanish perspective: Michael Rohrschneider, *Der gescheiterte Frieden von Münster. Spaniens Ringen mit Frankreich auf dem Westfälischen Friedenskongress (1643–1649)* (Münster, 2007). See also Dickmann, *Der Westfälische Frieden*; Westphal, *Der Westfälische Frieden*; Repgen, 'Hauptprobleme'; Croxton, *Last Christian Peace*.

42. E.g. protocol (minutes) of the electors, 19 March 1646, in APW III 1/1 (Münster, 1975), 535ff. See also Dickmann, *Der Westfälische Frieden*, 332–43.
43. Fritz Dickmann, 'Rechtsgedanke und Machtpolitik bei Richelieu. Studien zu neuentdeckten Quellen', in Fritz Dickmann, *Friedensrecht und Friedenssicherung. Studien zum Friedensproblem in der Geschichte* (Göttingen, 1971), 36–78; Hermann Weber, '"Une bonne paix": Richelieu's foreign policy and the peace of Christendom', in Joseph Bergin and Laurence Brockliss, eds., *Richelieu and his Age* (Oxford, 1992), 45–69.
44. See the main French instructions for its plenipotentiaries at Münster: APW I 1, ed. Fritz Dickmann et al. (Münster, 1962), 58–123.
45. Guido Braun, 'Die französische Diplomatie und das Problem der Friedenssicherung auf dem Westfälischen Friedenskongress', in Guido Braun, *Assecuratio Pacis. Französische Konzeptionen von Friedenssicherung und Friedensgarantie 1648–1815* (Münster, 2011), 67–130.
46. APW II A 9, May–August 1648, ed. Stefanie Fraedrich-Nowag (Münster, 2013), 332. This shows that there was not much opposition to the notion of treaty enforcement and the concomitant risk of intervention in principle; instead the actors wished to create opportunities for legally grounded interventions by presumed allies, as they assumed that the power-political alignments of the Thirty Years War would probably persist in post-war geopolitical constellations.
47. Maria-Elisabeth Brunert, 'Friedenssicherung als Beratungsthema der protestantischen Reichsstände in der Schlussphase des Westfälischen Friedenskongresses', in Guido Braun and Arno Strohmeyer, eds., *Frieden und Friedenssicherung in der Frühen Neuzeit. Das Heilige Römische Reich und Europa. Festschrift für Maximilian Lanzinner* (Münster, 2013), 229–58; Ruppert, *Kaiserliche Politik*, 107, 117.
48. IPO, Art. 5, § 34: Clive Parry, ed., *Consolidated Treaty Series*, vol. 1 (Dobbs Ferry, 1969), 228–9.
49. Volker Arnke, 'Implementing the 1648 religious agreements in practice: Confessional conflict and co-existence in the prince-bishopric of Osnabrück—a case study', unpublished paper presented at seminar 4 of 'A Westphalia for the Middle East', London, 11 May 2016.
50. Quoted in Simms, *Europe*, 39.
51. Wilson, *The Holy Roman Empire*, 127.
52. Volker Press, 'Die kaiserliche Stellung im Reich zwischen 1648 und 1740—Versuch einer Neubewertung', in Georg Schmidt, ed., *Stände und Gesellschaften im Alten Reich* (Stuttgart, 1989), 51–80.
53. Croxton, *Last Christian Peace*, 361.
54. Heinhard Steiger, 'Der Westfälische Frieden—Grundgesetz für Europa?', in Heinz Duchhardt, ed., *Der Westfälische Friede. Diplomatie, politische Zäsur, kulturelles Umfeld, Rezeptionsgeschichte* (Munich, 1998), 33–80. See also Croxton, *Last Christian Peace*, 363.

55. See Patrick Milton, 'The mutual guarantee of the Peace of Westphalia in the law of nations and its impact on European diplomacy', forthcoming in *Journal of the History of International Law*.
56. Philalethus Archistor, *Raisonnement. Reiff-erwogenes Staats-Bedencken, wie beede Cronen Franckreich und Schweden unter dem Praetext der im Instrumento Pacis ihnen überlassenen Garantie dem Römischen Reich höchstnachtheilige Dinge favoriren; wie solche durch Ihre Entreprises sattsam erkannt, und mit was für Raison und Glück sie bißhero werckstellig gemacht und fortgesetzet worden* (1676), also in *Materialien und Beyträge zur Geschichte, den Rechten und deren Litteratur. Stück 2*, ed. Carl Friedrich Häberlin (Erlangen, 1785), 206–31.
57. Anuschka Tischer, *Offizielle Kriegsbegründungen in der Frühen Neuzeit: Herrscherkommunikation in Europa zwischen Souveränität und korporativem Selbstverständnis* (Münster 2012), 140–1.
58. *An Ihro Roem. Kayserliche ... Majestät Josephum I. Der Augspurgischen Confessions-Verwandten Churfürsten/ Fürsten und Stände ... Fernere Intercessionales, für Ihre Glaubens=Genossen im Herzogthum Schlesien* (Regensburg, 5 June 1708).
59. Joachim Whaley, *Germany and the Holy Roman Empire* (Oxford, 2012), vol. 1, 640.
60. Joachim Whaley, 'A tolerant society? Religious toleration in the Holy Roman Empire, 1648–1806', in Ole Peter Grell and Roy Porter, eds., *Toleration in Enlightenment Europe* (Cambridge, 2000), 175–95.
61. Andrew C. Thompson, 'The maintenance of the confessional peace', unpublished paper presented at seminar 4 of 'A Westphalia for the Middle East', London, 11 May 2016.
62. Quoted in Patrick Milton, 'The early eighteenth-century German confessional crisis: The juridification of religious conflict in the re-confessionalised politics of the Holy Roman Empire', *Central European History*, 49, no. 1 (2016), 39–68 at 53.
63. Patrick Milton, 'Guarantee and intervention: The assessment of the Peace of Westphalia in international law and politics by authors of natural law and of public law, c.1650–1806', in Simone Zurbuchen, ed., *The Law of Nations and Natural Law, 1625–1850* (Leiden, forthcoming).

5. PARALLELS AND ANALOGIES

1. Quoted in Derek Croxton, *The Last Christian Peace: The Congress of Westphalia as a Baroque Event* (Basingstoke, 2013), 1.
2. Quoted in the report *Reinventing 'Westphalia': Historical Lessons for a future peace in the Middle East*, Körber-Stiftung, 2017, 10–11.
3. Herfried Münkler, *Der Dreissigjährige Krieg. Europäische Katastrophe, deutsches Trauma, 1618–1648* (Berlin, 2017), 828ff; 'Der Festgeschnürte Frieden: Prof.

Christoph Kampmann erklärt ein Meisterwerk der Diplomatie', *P.M. History*, May 2017.

4. Saeed Kamali Dehghan, 'Aden crisis: Alliances of convenience unravel across Yemen', *The Guardian*, 30 Jan. 2018.
5. Anthony H. Cordesmann, 'Iraq: The enemy of my enemy is not my friend', *Center for Strategic and International Studies*, 16 July 2014, https://www.csis.org/analysis/iraq-enemy-my-enemy-not-my-friend; Sara Elizabeth Williams, 'Turkey launches ground offensive in northern Syria against US-backed militias', *The Telegraph*, 21 Jan. 2018.
6. Peter Wilson, 'The character of the Thirty Years War', unpublished paper presented at seminar 2 of 'A Westphalia for the Middle East', Cambridge, 19 March 2016.
7. Georg Schmidt, *Der Dreissigjährige Krieg* (Munich, 2010), 32.
8. Kampmann, *Europa und das Reich*, 83, 140; Croxton, *Last Christian Peace*, 109.
9. Kampmann, *Europa und das Reich*, 55.
10. Croxton, *Last Christian Peace*, 65.
11. For the role of exiles, see Alexander Schunka, 'Böhmische Exulanten in Sachsen seit dem 17. Jahrhundert', in Klaus J. Bade, Pieter C. Emmer, Leo Lucassen and Jochen Oltmer, eds., *Enzyklopädie Migration in Europa. Vom 17. Jahrhundert bis zur Gegenwart* (Paderborn, 2007), 410–13; Alexander Schunka, 'Exulanten, Konvertiten, Arme und Fremde. Zuwanderer aus der Habsburgermonarchie in Kursachsen im 17. Jahrhundert', *Frühneuzeit-Info*, 14 (2003), 66–78; Michael Kagan, 'Decade of exile: Syria and the Middle East's refugee crisis', *World Politics Review*, 23 June 2015, https://www.worldpoliticsreview.com/articles/16070/decade-of-exile-syria-and-the-middle-east-s-refugee-crisis; Shirine Saad, 'The distant imagination of the Middle East's exiled writers', *The National*, 9 January 2014, https://www.thenational.ae/arts-culture/the-distant-imagination-of-the-middle-east-s-exiled-writers-1.326742.
12. Yochi Dreazen, 'Meet the weird, super-connected group that's mucking up U.S. talks with Iraq', *Foreign Policy*, 30 Oct. 2013, http://foreignpolicy.com/2013/10/30/meet-the-weird-super-connected-group-thats-mucking-up-u-s-talks-with-iraq/#.UnF7tJ867nE.twitter.
13. As argued by John Jenkins, 'The new great game in the Middle East', *New Statesman*, 24 Nov. 2017.
14. Croxton, *Last Christian Peace*, 361.
15. Johannes Burkhardt, *Der Dreißigjährige Krieg* (Frankfurt, 1992).
16. For IS and jihadi state-building, see Brynjar Lia, 'Understanding Jihadi proto-states', *Perspectives on Terrorism*, 9, no. 4 (2015), 31–41; Cole Bunzel, 'From paper state to caliphate: The ideology of the Islamic State', *The Brookings Project on U.S. Relations with the Islamic World*, Analysis Paper, no. 19, March 2015; Connor Kopchick, 'Jihadi state-building: A comparative study of Jihadis' capacity for gov-

ernance', 7 Dec. 2015, http://www.e-ir.info/2015/12/07/jihadi-state-building-a-comparative-study-of-jihadis-capacity-for-governance/.

17. Tim Black, 'The apocalyptic barbarism of ISIS', *Spiked*, 27 Nov. 2017, http://www.spiked-online.com/newsite/article/the-apocalyptic-barbarism-of-isis-egypt-sinai/20581#.WnDzlOdG3V8.
18. Anuschka Tischer, 'Vom Kriegsgrund hin zum Friedensschluß: der Einfluß unterschiedlicher Faktoren auf die Formulierung von Friedensverträgen am Beispiel des Westfälischen Friedens', in Heinz Duchhardt and Martin Peters, eds., *Kalkül—Transfer—Symbol. Europäische Friedensverträge der Vormoderne* (Mainz, 2 Nov. 2006), www.ieg-mainz.de/vieg-online-beihefte/01-2006.html, section 100.
19. Heinz Schilling, *Konfessionalisierung und Staatsinteressen. Internationale Beziehungen 1559–1660* (Paderborn, 2007), 477–98.
20. Michael Axworthy, 'Sunni vs. Shia: The roots of Islam's civil war', *New Statesman*, 29 Aug. 2017, https://www.newstatesman.com/world/middle-east/2017/08/sunni-vs-shia-roots-islam-s-civil-war; Tom Wilson, 'Foreign funded Islamist extremism in the UK', Henry Jackson Society/Centre for the Response to Radicalisation and Terrorism Research Paper no. 9 (2017), http://henryjacksonsociety.org/2017/07/05/foreign-funded-islamist-extremism-in-the-uk/.
21. Wilson, *Europe's Tragedy*, 221–3.
22. Cornel Zwierlein, 'The Thirty Years War: A religious war? Religion and Machiavellism at the turning point of 1635', in Olaf Asbach and Peter Schröder, eds., *The Ashgate Research Companion to the Thirty Years War* (Farnham, 2014), 231–45.
23. Quoted in Croxton, *Last Christian Peace*, 346.
24. Bård Kårtveit and Maria Gabrielsen Jumbert, 'Civil-military relations in the Middle East: A literature review', Chr. Michelsen Institute Working Paper (Bergen, 2014); Ahmed Abd Rabou, *Civil-Military Relations in the Middle East: A Comparative Study of the Political Role of the Military in Egypt and Turkey* (Paris, 2016).
25. Kampmann, *Europa und das Reich*, 181.
26. Christoph Kampmann, *Reichsrebellion und kaiserliche Acht. Politische Strafjustiz im Dreißigjährigen Krieg und das Verfahren gegen Wallenstein 1634* (Münster, 1992), 101ff.
27. Lisa Anderson, 'Absolutism and the resilience of monarchy in the Middle East', *Political Science Quarterly*, 106, no. 1 (1991), 1–15; F. Gregory Gause and Sean L. Yom, 'Resilient royals: How Arab monarchies hang on', *Journal of Democracy*, 23, no. 4 (2012), 74–88.
28. UNHCR report on Syrian emergency, http://www.unhcr.org/pages/5051e8cd6.html.
29. Schmidt, *Der Dreissigjährige Krieg*, 92.
30. Alexandra Siegel, 'Sectarian Twitter wars: Sunni-Shia conflict and cooperation in the digital age', *Carnegie Endowment for International Peace*, 20 Dec. 2015, http://

carnegieendowment.org/2015/12/20/sectarian-twitter-wars-sunni-shia-conflict-and-cooperation-in-digital-age-pub-62299.

31. Croxton, *Last Christian Peace*, 380; Anuschka Tischer, *Offizielle Kriegsbegründungen in der Frühen Neuzeit. Herrscherkommunikation in Europa zwischen Souveränität und korporativem Selbstverständnis* (Münster 2012), 58–78 et passim; Westphal, *Der Westfälische Frieden*, 13.
32. Geoffrey Parker, *Global Crisis: War, Climate Change and Catastrophe in the Seventeenth Century*, part 1 (New Haven, 2014).
33. Ryan Jacobs, 'Saudi Arabia's war on witchcraft', *The Atlantic*, 19 Aug. 2013, https://www.theatlantic.com/international/archive/2013/08/saudi-arabias-war-on-witchcraft/278701; Richard Spencer, 'Isil carried out massacres and mass sexual enslavement of Yazidis, UN confirms', *The Telegraph*, 14 Oct. 2014, https://www.telegraph.co.uk/news/worldnews/islamic-state/11160906/Isil-carried-out-massacres-and-mass-sexual-enslavement-of-Yazidis-UN-confirms.html; Harriet Sherwood, 'Christians in Egypt face unprecedented persecution, report says', *The Guardian*, 10 Jan. 2018, https://www.theguardian.com/world/2018/jan/10/christians-egypt-unprecedented-persecution-report.

6. LESSONS FOR THE MIDDLE EAST: PEACEMAKING MECHANISMS, DIPLOMATIC TECHNIQUES AND A NEW REGIONAL ORDER

1. Quoted in the report *Reinventing 'Westphalia': Historical Lessons for a Future Peace in the Middle East*, Körber-Stiftung, 2017, 2.
2. Quoted in ibid., 2.
3. Quoted in ibid., 11.
4. Galip Dalay, 'Break-up of the Middle East: Will we see a new regional order?', *Middle East Eye*, 22 Aug. 2017, http://www.middleeasteye.net/essays/middle-east-fragmentation-opportunity-regional-co-operation-1111336507.
5. Croxton, *Last Christian Peace*, 333.
6. Weber, '"Une bonne paix". Richelieu's foreign policy and the peace of Christendom', 45–69.
7. Anuschka Tischer, 'Vom Kriegsgrund hin zum Friedensschluß. Der Einfluß unterschiedlicher Faktoren auf die Formulierung von Friedensverträgen am Beispiel des Westfälischen Friedens', in Heinz Duchhardt and Martin Peters, eds., *Kalkül—Transfer—Symbol. Europäische Friedensverträge der Vormoderne* (Mainz, 2 Nov. 2006), www.ieg-mainz.de/vieg-online-beihefte/01–2006.html, sec. 108.
8. Konrad Repgen, 'Die Hauptprobleme der WestfälischenFriedensverhandlungen von 1648 und ihre Lösungen', *Zeitschrift für bayerische Landesgeschichte*, 62 (1999), 399–438.
9. Peter H. Wilson, *The Thirty Years War: A Sourcebook* (Basingstoke, 2010), 280.
10. Michael Rohrschneider, *Der gescheiterte Frieden von Münster. Spaniens Ringen*

mit Frankreich auf dem Westfälischen Friedenskongress (1643–1649) (Münster, 2007), 384.

11. Michael Rohrschneider, 'Tradition und Perzeption als Faktoren in den internationalen Beziehungen. Das Beispiel der wechselseitigen Wahrnehmung der französischen und spanischen Politik auf dem westfälischen Friedenskongreß', *Zeitschrift für historische Forschung*, 29 (2002), 257–82.
12. For mediation in early modern Europe, see Christoph Kampmann, 'Friedensstiftung von außen? Die Problematik von Friedensvermittlung und Schiedsgerichtsbarkeit in frühneuzeitlichen Staatenkonflikten', in Claudia Ulbrich, Claudia Jarzebowski and Michaela Hochkamp, eds., *Gewalt in der Frühen Neuzeit* (Berlin, 2005), 245–59.
13. Quoted in Rohrschneider, *Der Gescheiterte Frieden von Münster*, 81.
14. On the role of trust in peacemaking negotiations, see Paul R. Pillar, *Negotiating Peace: War Termination as a Bargaining Process* (Princeton, 1983), 80–2.
15. Croxton, *Last Christian Peace*, 375.
16. Ibid., 370–2.
17. Ibid., 383; Rohrschneider, *Der Gescheiterte Frieden von Münster*, 373ff.
18. Ruppert, *Kaiserliche Politik*, 361.
19. Croxton, *Last Christian Peace*, 381.
20. Maria-Elisabeth Brunert, 'Seeking peace through negotiations, mediation and settlement, 1640–1650', unpublished paper presented at seminar 3 of 'A Westphalia for the Middle East', Cambridge, 23 April 2016.
21. Dickmann, *Der Westfälische Frieden*, 149–53, 157–63, 169–72, 332–6, 339–43.
22. Antje Ochsmann, *Der Nürnberger Exekutionstag, 1649–1650. Das Ende des Dreißigjährigen Krieges in Deutschland* (Münster, 1991).
23. 'Der Festgeschnürte Frieden: Prof. Christoph Kampmann erklärt ein Meisterwerk der Diplomatie', *P.M. History*, May 2017.
24. Quoted in the report *Reinventing 'Westphalia': Historical Lessons for a Future Peace in the Middle East*, 2.
25. 'Was der Dreißigjährige Krieg mit heutigen Kriegen zu tun hat', *Siegel Online* interview by Jan Fleischhauer and Cordula Meyer with Herfried Münkler, http://www.spiegel.de/spiegel/herfried-muenkler-ueber-den-dreissigjaehrigen-krieg-a-1175447.html; 'Mit Maria kämpft's sich leichter', *Die Zeit* interview by Raol Löbbert and Fabian Klask with Herfried Münkler, http://www.zeit.de/2017/47/herfried-muenkler-dreissigjaehriger-krieg-reformationsjahr/komplettansicht; Croxton, *Last Christian Peace*, 280, 369.

INDEX